Sir William Hamilton

An Account of the remains of the worship of Priapus

Sir William Hamilton

An Account of the remains of the worship of Priapus

ISBN/EAN: 9783337273569

Printed in Europe, USA, Canada, Australia, Japan

Cover: Foto ©Andreas Hilbeck / pixelio.de

More available books at **www.hansebooks.com**

AN

ACCOUNT OF THE REMAINS

OF THE

WORSHIP

OF

PRIAPUS,

LATELY EXISTING AT

ISERNIA, in the Kingdom of *NAPLES*:

IN TWO LETTERS;

One from Sir WILLIAM HAMILTON, K.B. His Majesty's Minister at the Court of *Naples*, to Sir JOSEPH BANKS, Bart. President of the Royal Society;

And the other from a Person residing at *Isernia*:

TO WHICH IS ADDED,

A DISCOURSE ON THE WORSHIP OF PRIAPUS,

And its Connexion with the mystic Theology of the Ancients.

By *R. P. KNIGHT*, Esq.

LONDON:
Printed by T. SPILSBURY, *Snowhill*.
M.DCC.LXXXVI.

A

L E T T E R

FROM

SIR *WILLIAM HAMILTON*, &c.

Naples, Dec. 30, 1781.

S I R,

HAVING laſt year made a curious diſcovery, that in a Province of this Kingdom, and not fifty miles from its Capital, a ſort of

 devo-

devotion is ſtill paid to PRIAPUS, the obſcene Divinity of the Ancients (though under another denomination), I thought it a circumſtance worth recording; particularly, as it offers a freſh proof of the ſimilitude of the Popiſh and Pagan Religion, ſo well obſerved by Doctor MIDDLETON, in his celebrated Letter from ROME: and therefore I mean to depoſit the authentic *proofs of this aſſertion in the BRITISH MUSEUM, when a proper opportunity ſhall offer. In the mean time I ſend you the following account, which, I flatter myſelf, will amuſe you for the preſent, and may in future ſerve to illuſtrate thoſe proofs.

I had long ago diſcovered, that the Women and Children of the lower claſs, at NAPLES, and in its neighbourhood, frequently wore, as an ornament of dreſs, ſort of Amulets, (which they imagine to be a preſervative from the *mal occhii*, *evil eyes*, or enchantment) exactly ſimilar to thoſe which were worn by the ancient Inhabitants of this Country for the very

* A ſpecimen of each of the *Ex-voti* of wax, with the original Letter from ISERNIA. See the Ex-voti, Plate I.

Plate 1

Ex Voti of Wax prefented to the Church at Isernia 1780

very ſame purpoſe, as likewiſe for their ſuppoſed invigorating influence; and all of which have evidently a relation to the Cult of PRIAPUS. Struck with this conformity in modern and ancient ſuperſtition, I made a collection of both the ancient and modern Amulets of this ſort, and placed them together in the BRITISH MUSEUM, where they remain. The modern Amulet moſt in vogue, repreſents a hand clinched, with the point of the thumb thruſt betwixt the index and middle *finger; the next is a ſhell; and the third is a half-moon. Theſe Amulets (except the ſhell, which is uſually worn in its natural ſtate) are moſt commonly made of ſilver, but ſometimes of ivory, coral, amber, cryſtal, or ſome curious gem, or pebble. We have a proof of the hand above deſcribed having a connexion with PRIAPUS, in a moſt elegant ſmall idol of bronze of that Divinity, now in the ROYAL MUSEUM of PORTICI, and which was found in the ruins of HERCULANEUM: it has an enormous Phallus, and, with an arch look and geſture, ſtretches out its right hand

---

* See Plate II. Fig. I. Vignette to this Letter.

hand in the form above mentioned*; and which probably was an emblem of consummation: and as a further proof of it, the Amulet which occurs most frequently amongst those of the Ancients (next to that which represents the simple Priapus, is such a hand united with the Phallus; of which you may see several specimens in my collection in the BRITISH MUSEUM. One in particular, I recollect, has also the half-moon joined to the hand and Phallus; which half-moon is supposed to have an allusion to the female *menses*. The shell, or *concha veneris*, is evidently an emblem of the female part of generation. It is very natural then to suppose, that the Amulets representing the Phallus alone, so visibly indecent, may have been long out of use in this civilized capital; but I have been assured, that it is but very lately that the Priests have put an end to the wearing of such Amulets in CALABRIA, and other distant Provinces of this Kingdom.

A new road having been made last year from this Capital to the Province of ABRUZZO, passing through the

* This elegant little Figure is engraved in the First Volume of the Bronzes of the Herculaneum.

the City of ISERNIA (anciently belonging to the SAMNITES, and very populous*), a person of a liberal education, employed in that work, chanced to be at ISERNIA just at the time of the celebration of the Feast of the modern PRIAPUS, St. COSMO; and having been struck with the singularity of the ceremony, so very similar to that which attended the ancient Cult of the GOD of the GARDENS, and knowing my taste for antiquities, told me of it. From this Gentleman's report, and from what I learnt on the spot from the Governor of ISERNIA himself, having gone to that City on purpose in the month of February last, I have drawn up the following account, which I have reason to believe is strictly true. I did intend to have been present at the Feast of St. COSMO this year; but the indecency of this ceremony having probably transpired, from the country's having been more frequented since the new road was made, orders have been given, that the *Great Toe*† of the Saint should no longer be exposed. The following

* The actual Population of ISERNIA, according to the Governor's account, is 5156.

† See the Italian letter, printed at the end of this, from which it appears the modern PRIAPI were so called at ISERNIA.

following is the account of the Fête of St. Cosmo and Damiano, as it actually was celebrated at Isernia, on the confines of Abruzzo, in the Kingdom of Naples, so late as in the year of our Lord 1780.

On the 27th of September, at Isernia, one of the most ancient cities of the Kingdom of Naples, situated in the Province called the Contado di Molise, and adjoining to Abruzzo, an annual Fair is held, which lasts three days. The situation of this Fair is on a rising ground, between two rivers, about half a mile from the town of Isernia; on the most elevated part of which there is an ancient Church, with a vestibule. The architecture is of the style of the lower ages; and it is said to have been a Church and Convent belonging to the Benedictine Monks in the time of their poverty. This Church is dedicated to St. Cosmus and Damianus. One of the days of the Fair, the relicks of the Saints are exposed, and afterwards carried in procession from the Cathedral of the City to this Church, attended by a prodigious concourse of people. In the city, and at the fair, *Ex-voti* of wax, representing the male parts of generation, of various

various dimenſions, ſome even of the length of a palm, are publickly offered to ſale. There are alſo waxen vows, that repreſent other parts of the body mixed with them; but of thoſe there are few in compariſon of the number of the Priapi. The devout diſtributers of theſe vows carry a baſket full of them in one hand, and hold a plate in the other to receive the money, crying aloud, "St. Cosmo "and Damiano!" If you aſk the price of one, the anſwer is, *più ci metti, più meriti:* "The "more you give, the more's the merit." In the Veſtibule are two tables, at each of which one of the Canons of the Church preſides, this crying out, *Qui ſi riceveno le Miſſe, e Litanie:* "Here Maſſes "and Litanies are received;" and the other, *Qui ſi riceveno li Voti:* "Here the Vows are received." The price of a Maſs is fifteen Neapolitan grains, and of a Litany five grains. On each table is a large baſon for the reception of the different offerings. The Vows are chiefly preſented by the female ſex; and they are ſeldom ſuch as repreſent legs, arms, &c. but moſt commonly the male parts of generation. The Perſon who was at this Fête in the year 1780, and who gave me this account (the authenticity of every article of which has ſince been fully confirmed to me by the Governor of ISERNIA), told me alſo, that he heard a Woman ſay at the time ſhe preſented a vow, like that which is repreſented in Plate I. Fig. I. *Santo Coſimo benedetto, coſi lo voglio:* "Bleſſed St. COSMO, let it be like this;" another, *St. Coſimo, a te mi raccommendo:* "St. COSMO, I "recommend myſelf to you;" and a third, *St. Coſimo, ti ringrazio:* "St. COSMO, I thank you." The Vow is never preſented without being accompanied by a piece of money, and is always kiſſed by the devotee at the moment of preſentation.

At the great Altar in the Church, another of its Canons attends to give the holy unction, with the oil of St. COSMO*; which is prepared by the ſame receipt as that of the Roman Ritual, with the addition only of the prayer of the Holy Martyrs, St. COSMUS

* The cure of diſeaſes by oil is likewiſe of ancient date; for TERTULLIAN tells us, that a Chriſtian, called PROCULUS, cured the Emperor SEVERUS of a certain diſtemper by the uſe of oil; for which ſervice the Emperor kept PROCULUS, as long as he lived, in his Palace.

Cosmus and Damianus. Those who have an infirmity in any of their members, present themselves at the great Altar, and uncover the member affected (not even excepting that which is most frequently represented by the *Ex-voti*); and the reverend Canon anoints it, saying, *Per intercessionem beati Cosmi, liberet te ab omni malo. Amen.*

The ceremony finishes by the Canons of the Church dividing the spoils, both money and wax, which must be to a very considerable amount, as the concourse at this Fête is said to be prodigiously numerous.

The Oil of St. Cosmo is in high repute for its invigorating quality, when the loins, and parts adjacent, are anointed with it. No less than 1400 flasks of that oil were either expended at the Altar in unctions, or charitably distributed during this Fête in the year 1780; and as it is usual for every one, who either makes use of the oil at the Altar, or carries off a flask of it, to leave an alms for St. Cosmo, the ceremony of the Oil becomes likewise a very lucrative one to the Canons of the Church.

I am, SIR,

with great truth and regard,

Your most obedient humble Servant,

William Hamilton.

Plate III.

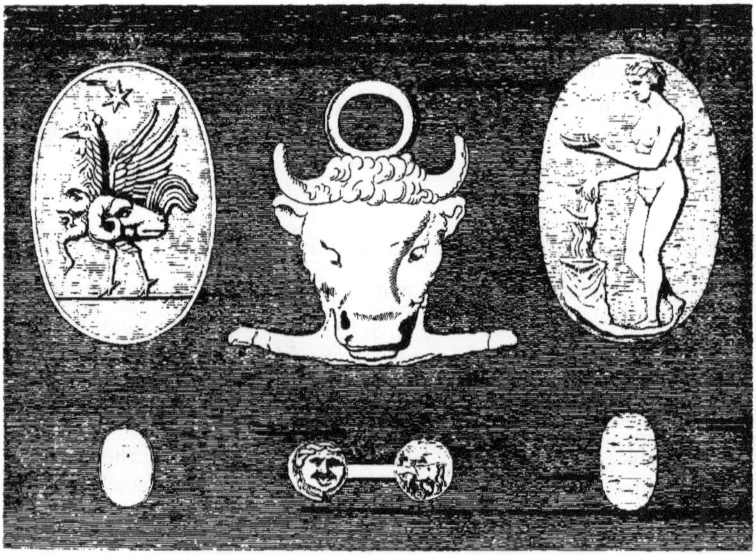

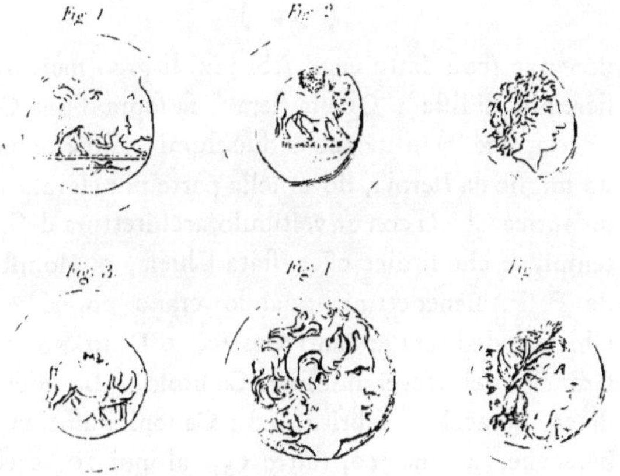

L E T T E R A
D A *I S E R N I A*,
NELL'ANNO 1780.

IN ISERNIA Città Sannitica, oggi della Provincia del Contado di Moliſe, ogni Anno li 27. Settembre vi è una Fiera della claſſe delle perdonanze

donanze (così dette negl' Abruzzi li gran mercati, e fiere non di lista): Questa fiera si fa sopra d'una Collinetta, che stà in mezzo a due fiumi; distante mezzo miglio da Isernia, dove nella parte piu elevata vi è un'antica Chiesa con un vestibulo, architettura de' bassi tempi, e che si dice esser stata Chiesa, e Monistero de P. P. Benedettini, quando erano poveri? La Chiesa è dedicata ai Santi Cosmo, e Damiano, ed è Grancia del Reverendissimo Capitolo. La Fiera è di 50. baracche a fabrica, ed i Canonici affittano le baracche, alcune 10, altre 15, al pui 20, carlini l'una; affittano ancora per tre giorni l'osteria fatta di fabbrica docati 20 ed i comestibili sono benedetti. Vi è un Eremita della stessa umanità del fù F. Glaud guardiano del Monte Vesuvio, cittato con rispetto dall' Ab. Richard. La fiera dura tre giorni. Il Maestro di fiera è il Capitolo, ma commette al Governatore Regio; e questo alza bandiera con l'impresa della Citta, che è la stessa impresa de P. P. Celestini. Si fa una Processione con le Reliquie dei Santi, ed esce dalla Cattedrale, e và alla Chiesa sudetta; ma è poco devota. Il giorno della festa, sì per la Città, come nella collinetta vi è un gran concorso d'Abitatori del Motese, Mainarde, ed altri

Monti

Monti vicini, che la ſtranezza delli veſtimenti delle Donne, ſembra, a chi non ha gl'occhi avvezzi avederle, il pui bel ridotto di maſcherate. Le Donne della Terra del Gallo ſono vere figlie dell'Ordine Serafico Cappuccino, veſtendo come li Zoccolanti in materia, e forma. Puelle di Scanno Sembrano Greche di Scio. Puelle di Carovilli Armene. Puelle delle Peſche, e Carpinone tengono ſul capo alcuni panni roſſi con ricamo di filo bianco, diſegno ſul guſto Etruſco che a pochi paſſi ſembra merletto d'Inghilterra. Vi è fra queſte Donne vera bellezza, e diverſità grande nel veſtire, anche fra due popolazioni viciniſſime, ed un attaccamento particolare di certe popolazioni ad un colore, ed altre ad altro. L'abito è diſtinto nelle Zitelle, Maritate, Vedove, è Donne di piacere?

Nella fiera, ed in Città vi ſono molti divoti, che vendono membri virili di cera di diverſe forme, e di tutte le grandezze, fino ad un palmo; e miſchiate vi ſono ancora gambe, braccia, e faccie; ma poche ſono queſte. Quei li vendono tengono un ceſto, ed un piatto; li membri rotti ſono nel ceſto, ed il piatto ſerve per raccogliere il danaro d'elemoſina.

Gridano

Gridano S. Cosmo e Damiano. Chi è ſprattico domanda, quanto un vale? Riſpondono *più ci metti, più meriti.* Avanti la Chieſa nel veſtibolo del Tempio vi ſono due tavole, ciaſcuna con ſedia, dove preſiede un Canonico, e ſuol' eſſere uno il Primicerio, e l'altro l'Arciprete: grida uno *qui ſi ricevono le Meſſe, e Litanie:* l'altro, *qui ſi ricevono li voti*; ſopra delle tavole in ogn'una vi è un bacile, che ſerve per raccogliere li membri di cera, che mai ſi preſentano ſoli, ma con denaro, come ſi è pratticato ſempre in tutte le preſentazioni di membri, ad eccezzione di quelli dell'Iſola di Ottaiti. Queſta divozione è tutta quaſi delle Donne, e ſono pochiſſimi quelli, o quelle che preſentano gambe, e braccia, mentre tutta la gran feſta s'aggira a profitto de membri della generazione. Io ho inteſo dire ad una donna. *Santo Coſimo benedetto, coſì lo voglio.* Altre dicevano, *Santo Coſimo a te mi raccommando:* altre, *Santo Coſimo ti ringrazio*; e queſto è quello oſſervai, e ſi prattica nel veſtibulo, baciando ogn'una il voto che preſente.

Dentro la Chieſa nell'altare maggiore un Canonico fa le ſante unzioni con l'olio di S. Coſimo. La

ricetta

ricetta di quest' olio è la stessa del Rituale Romano, con l'aggiunta dell'orazione delli S. S. Martiri Cosimo, e Damiano. Si presentano all' Altare gl'Infermi d'ogni male, snudano la parte offesa, anche l'originale della copia di cera, ed il Canonico ungendoli dice, *Per intercessionem beati Cosmi, liberet te ab omni malo. Amen.*

Finisce la festa con dividersi li Canonici la cera, ed il denaro, e con ritornar gravide molte Donne sterili maritate, a profitto della popolazione delle Provincie ; e spesso la grazia s'estende senza meraviglia, alle Zitelle, e Vedove, che per due notti hanno dormito, alcune nella Chiesa de' P. P. Zoccolanti, ed altre delli Cappuccini, non essendoci in Isernia Case locande per alloggiare tutto il numero di gente, che concorre : onde li Frati, ajutando ai Preti, danno le Chiese alle Donne, ed i Portici agl' Uomini ; e così Divisi succedendo gravidanze non deve dubitar si, che si a opera tutta miracolosa, e di divozione.

NOTA I.

L'olio non solo serve per l'unzione che fà il Canonico, ma anche si dispensa in picciolissime caraffine,

 e serve

e ſerve per ungerſi li lombi a chi ha male a queſta parte. In queſt' anno 1780. ſi ſono date par divozione 1400. caraſine, e ſi è conſumato mezzo Stajo d'olio. Chi prende una caraffina dà l'olemoſina.

NOTA II.

Li Canonici che ſiedono nel Veſtibulo prendono denaro d' Elemoſina per Meſſe, e per Litanie. Le Meſſea grana 15. e le litanie a grana 5.

NOTA III.

Li foreſtieri alloggiano non ſolo frà li Cappuccini e Zoccolanti, ma anche nell' Eramo di S. Coſmo. Le donne che Dormono nelle chieſe de' P. P. Sudetti ſono guardate dalli Guardiani, Vicarj e Padri piu di merito, e quelli dell' Eremo ſono in cura dell'Eremita, diviſe anche dai Proprj Mariti, e ſi fanno ſpeſſo miracoli ſenza incomodo delli ſanti:

Se non

Se non le gusta, quando l'avrà letta
Tornerà bene farne una baldoria :
Che le daranno almen qualche diletto
Le Monachine quando vanno a letto.

Plate V.

ON THE

WORSHIP

OF

PRIAPUS.

MEN, considered collectively, are at all times the same animals, employing the same organs, and endowed with the same faculties: their passions, prejudices,

prejudices, and conceptions, will of courfe be formed upon the fame internal principles, although directed to various ends, and modified in various ways, by the variety of external circumftances operating upon them. Education and fcience may correct, reftrain, and extend; but neither can annihilate or create: they may turn and embellifh the currents; but can neither ftop nor enlarge the fprings, which, continuing to flow with a perpetual and equal tide, return to their ancient channels, when the caufes that perverted them are withdrawn.

The firft principles of the human mind will be more directly brought into action, in proportion to the earneftnefs and affection with which it contemplates its object; and paffion and prejudice will acquire dominion over it, in proportion as its firft principles are more directly brought into action. On all common fubjects, this dominion of paffion and prejudice is reftrained by the evidence of fenfe and perception; but, when the mind is led to the contemplation of things beyond its comprehenfion, all fuch reftraints vanifh: reafon has then nothing to oppofe to the phantoms of imagination, which acquire terrors from their obfcurity, and dictate uncontrolled,

uncontrolled, becauſe unknown. Such is the caſe in all Religious ſubjects, which, being beyond the reach of ſenſe or reaſon, are always embraced or rejected with violence and heat. Men think they know, becauſe they are ſure they feel; and are firmly convinced, becauſe ſtrongly agitated. Hence proceed that haſte and violence with which devout perſons of all religions condemn the rites and doctrines of others, and the furious zeal and bigotry with which they maintain their own; while perhaps, if both were equally well underſtood, both would be found to have the ſame meaning, and only to differ in the modes of conveying it.

Of all the prophane rites which belonged to the ancient Polytheiſm, none were more furiouſly inveighed againſt by the zealous propagators of the Chriſtian faith, than the obſcene ceremonies performed in the worſhip of PRIAPUS; which appeared not only contrary to the gravity and ſanctity of religion, but ſubverſive of the firſt principles of decency and good order in ſociety. Even the form itſelf, under which the God was repreſented, appeared to them a mockery of all piety and devotion, and more fit to be placed in a brothel than a temple.

But

But the forms and ceremonials of a religion are not always to be underſtood in their direct and obvious ſenſe; but are to be conſidered as ſymbolical repreſentations of ſome hidden meaning, which may be extremely wiſe and juſt, though the ſymbols themſelves, to thoſe who know not their true ſignification, may appear in the higheſt degree abſurd and extravagant. It has often happened, that avarice and ſuperſtition have continued theſe ſymbolical repreſentations for ages after their original meaning has been loſt and forgotten; when they muſt of courſe appear nonſenſical and ridiculous, if not impious and extravagant.

Such is the caſe with the rite now under conſideration, than which nothing can be more monſtrous and indecent, if conſidered in its plain and obvious meaning, or as a part of the Chriſtian worſhip; but which will be found to be a very natural ſymbol of a very natural and philoſophical ſyſtem of religion, if conſidered according to its original uſe and intention.

What this was, I ſhall endeavour in the following ſheets to explain as conciſely and clearly as poſſible.

Thoſe

Thoſe who wiſh to know how generally the ſymbol, and the religion which it repreſented, once prevailed, will conſult the great and elaborate work of Mr. D'HANCARVILLE, who, with infinite learning and ingenuity, has traced its progreſs over the whole earth. My endeavour will be merely to ſhow, from what original principles in the human mind it was firſt adopted, and how it was connected with the ancient theology: matters of very curious enquiry, which will ſerve, better perhaps than any others, to illuſtrate that truth, which ought to be preſent in every man's mind when he judges of the actions of others, *that in morals, as well as phyſics, there is no effect without an adequate cauſe.* If in doing this, I frequently find it neceſſary to differ in opinion with the learned Author above mentioned, it will be always with the utmoſt deference and reſpect; as it is to him that we are indebted for the only reaſonable method of explaining the emblematical works of the ancient artiſts.

Whatever the Greeks and Egyptians meant by the ſymbol in queſtion, it was certainly nothing ludicrous or licentious; of which we need no other proof, than its having been carried in ſolemn proceſſion at the celebration of thofe myfteries in which the firft principles of their religion, the knowledge of the God of Nature, the Firft, the Supreme, the Intellectual*, were preferved free from the vulgar fuperftitions, and communicated, under the ftricteft oaths of fecrecy, to the iniated; who were obliged to purify themfelves, prior to their initiation, by abftaining from venery, and all impure food*. We may therefore be affured, that no impure meaning could be conveyed by this fymbol; but that it reprefented fome fundamental principle of their faith. What this was, it is difficult to obtain any direct information, on account of the fecrecy under which this part of their religion was guarded. PLUTARCH tells us, that the Egyptians reprefented OSIRIS with the organ of generation erect, to fhow his generative and prolific power: he alfo tells us, that OSIRIS was the fame Deity as the BACCHUS of the Greek mythology; who was alfo the fame as the firft-begotten Love (Ερως πρωτογονος) of ORPHEUS and HESIOD.* This Deity is celebrated by the ancient Poets as the Creator of all things, the Father of Gods and

---

* PLUT. de *If.* et *Of.*

and Men*; and it appears, by the paſſage above referred to, that the organ of generation was the ſymbol of his great characteriſtic attribute. This is perfectly conſiſtent with the general practice of the Greek artiſts, who (as will be made appear hereafter) uniformly repreſented the attributes of the Deity by the correſponding properties obſerved in the objects of ſight. They thus perſonified the epithets and titles applied to him in the hymns and litanies, and conveyed their ideas of him by forms, only intelligible to the initiated, inſtead of ſounds, which were intelligible to all. The organ of generation repreſented the generative or creative attribute, and, in the language of Painting and Sculpture, ſignified the ſame as the epithet παγγενετης, in the Orphic litanies..

This interpretation will perhaps ſurpriſe thoſe who have not been accuſtomed to diveſt their minds of the prejudices of education and faſhion; but I doubt not, but it will appear juſt and reaſonable to thoſe who conſider manners and cuſtoms as relative

* Orph. *Argon.* 422.

to the natural cauſes which produced them, rather than to the artificial opinions and prejudices of any particular age or country. There is naturally no impurity or licentiouſneſs in the moderate and regular gratification of any natural appetite; the turpitude conſiſting wholly in the exceſs or perverſion. Neither are the organs of one ſpecies of enjoyment naturally to be conſidered as ſubjects of ſhame and concealment more than thoſe of another; every refinement of modern manners on this head being derived from acquired habit, not from nature: habit, indeed long eſtabliſhed; for it ſeems to have been as general in Homer's days as at preſent; but which certainly did not exiſt when the myſtic ſymbols of the ancient worſhip were firſt adopted. As theſe ſymbols were intended to expreſs abſtract ideas by objects of ſight, the contrivers of them naturally ſelected thoſe objects whoſe characteriſtic properties ſeemed to have the greateſt analogy with the divine attributes which they wiſhed to repreſent. In an age, therefore, when no prejudices of artificial decency exiſted, what more juſt and natural image could they find, by which to expreſs their idea of the beneficent power of the great Creator, than that organ which endowed them with the power of procreation,

creation, and made them partakers, not only of the felicity of the Deity, but of his great characteristic attribute, that of multiplying his own image, communicating his blessings, and extending them to generations yet unborn?

In the ancient theology of GREECE, preserved in the Orphic Fragments, this Deity, the Ερως πρωτογονος, or first-begotten Love, is said to have been produced, together with Æther, by Time, or Eternity, (Κρονος) and Necessity, (Αναγκη) operating upon inert matter, (Χαος). He is described as eternally begetting, (αειγενητης); the Father of Night, called in later times, the lucid or splendid, (Φανης), because he first appeared in splendour; of a double nature, (διφυης), as possessing the general power of creation and generation, both active and passive, both male and female*. Light is

* ORPH. *Argon.* Ver. 12. This Poem of the Argonautic Expedition is not of the ancient ORPHEUS, but written in his name by some Poet posterior to HOMER; as appears by the allusion to ORPHEUS's descent into Hell; a Fable invented after the Homeric times. It is however of very great antiquity, as both the style and manner sufficiently prove; and, I think, cannot be later than the age of PISISTRATUS, to which it has

is his neceſſary and primary attribute, coeternal with himſelf, and with him brought forth from inert

has been generally attributed. The paſſage here refered to is cited from another Poem, which, at the time this was written, paſſed for a genuine work of the Thracian Bard: whether juſtly or not, matters little; for its being thought ſo at that time, proves it to be of the remoteſt antiquity. The other Orphic Poems cited in this Diſcourſe, are the Hymns, or Litanies, which are attributed by the early Chriſtian, and later Platonic Writers, to ONOMACRITUS, a Poet of the age of PISISTRATUS; but which are probably of various authors: (See BRUCKER. *Hiſt. Crit. Philoſ.* Vol. I. note 2. lib. I. c. 1.) They contain however nothing which proves them to be later than the Trojan times; and if ONOMACRITUS, or any later author, had any thing to do with them, it ſeems to have been only in new-verſifying them, and changing the dialect. (See GESNER. *Proleg. Orphica*, p. 26.) Had he forged them, and attempted to impoſe them upon the world, as the genuine compoſitions of an ancient bard, there can be no doubt, but that he would have ſtuffed them with antiquated words, and obſolete phraſes; which is by no means the caſe, the language being pure, and worthy the age of PISISTRATUS. Theſe poems are not properly hymns, for the hymns of the Greeks contained the nativities and actions of the Gods, like thoſe of HOMER and CALLIMACHUS; but theſe are compoſitions of a different kind, and are properly invocations or prayers uſed in the Orphic Myſteries, and ſeem nearly of the ſame claſs as the Pſalms of the Hebrews. The reaſon why they are ſo ſeldom mentioned by any of the early writers, and ſo perpetually referred to by the later, is that they belonged to the myſtic worſhip, where every thing was kept concealed under the ſtricteſt oaths of ſecrecy. But after the riſe of Chriſtianity, this ſacred ſilence was broken by the Greek converts, who revealed every thing which they thought

inert matter by necessity. Hence the purity and sanctity always attributed to light by the Greeks.* He

thought would depreciate the old religion, or recommend the new; whilst the Heathen Priests revealed whatever they thought would have a contrary tendency; and endeavoured to show, by publishing the real mystic creed of their religion, that the principles of it were not so absurd as its outward structure seemed to infer; but that, when stripped of poetical allegory and vulgar fable, their theology was pure, reasonable, and sublime. (GESNER. *Proleg. Orphica.*) The collection of these Poems now extant, being probably compiled and versified by several hands, with some forged, and others interpolated and altered, must be read with great caution; more especially the fragments preserved by the Fathers of the Church and Ammonian Platonics; for these writers made no scruple of forging any monuments of antiquity which suited their purposes; particularly the former, who, in addition to their natural zeal, having the interests of a confederate body to support, thought every means by which they could benefit that body, by extending the lights of revelation, and gaining proselytes to the true faith, not only allowable, but meritorious. (See CLEMENTINA, Hom. VII. sect. 10, RECOGN. Lib. I. sect. 65. ORIGEN. *apud Hieronom. Apolog.* 1 *contra Ruf.* et CHRYSOSTOM. *de Sacerdot.* Lib. I. CHRYSOSTOM in particular, not only justifies, but warmly commends, any frauds that can be practised for the advantage of the Church of Christ.) PAUSANIAS says, (Lib. IX.) that the Hymns of ORPHEUS were few and short; but next in poetical merit to those of HOMER, and superior to them in sanctity, (θεολογικωτεροι). These are probably the same as the genuine part of the collection now extant; but they are so intermixed, that it is difficult

* See SOPHOCL. *Oedip. Tyr.* Ver. 1436.

He is called the Father of Night, becaufe, by attracting the light to himfelf, and becoming the fountain which diftributed it to the world, he produced Night, which

---

difficult to fay, which are genuine, and which are not. Perhaps there is no furer rule for judging, than to compare the epithets and allegories with the fymbols and monograms on the Greek medals, and to make their agreement the teft of authenticity. The medals were the public acts and records of the State, made under the direction of the Magiftrates, who were generally initiated into the myfteries. We may therefore be affured, that whatever theological and mythological allufions are found upon them, were part of the ancient religion of GREECE. It is from thefe that many of the Orphic hymns and fragments are proved to contain the pure theology, or myftic faith of the ancients; which is called Orphic by PAUSANIAS, (Lib. I. c. 39) and which is fo unlike the vulgar religion, or poetical mythology, that one can fcarcely imagine, at firft fight, that it belonged to the fame people; but which will neverthelefs appear, upon accurate inveftigation, to be the fource from whence it flowed, and the caufe of all its extravagance.

The hiftory of ORPHEUS himfelf is fo confufed and obfcured by fable, that it is impoffible to obtain any certain information concerning him. According to general tradition, he was a Thracian, and introduced the myfteries, in which a more pure fyftem of religion was taught, into GREECE. (BRUCKER. Vol. I. Part 2. Lib. I. c. 1.) He is alfo faid to have travelled into EGYPT (DIODOR. SIC. Lib. I. p. 80.); but as the Egyptians pretended that all foreigners received their fciences from them, at a time when all foreigners who entered the country were put to death or enflaved, (DIODOR. SIC. Lib. I. p. 78, et 107.) this account may be rejected, with many others of the fame kind. The Egyptians certainly

which is called eternally-begotten, becauſe it had eternally exiſted, although mixed and loſt in the general maſs. He is ſaid to pervade the world with the motion of his wings, bringing pure light; and thence to be called the ſplendid, the ruling PRIAPUS, and ſelf-illumined (αυταυγης†). It is to be obſerved, that the word Πριηπος, afterwards the name of a ſubordinate deity, is here uſed as a title relating to one of his attributes; the reaſons for which I ſhall endeavour

 to

---

certainly could not have taught ORPHEUS the plurality of worlds, and true ſolar ſyſtem, which appear to have been the fundamental principles of his philoſophy and religion (PLUTARCH. *de Placit. Philoſ.* Lib. II. c. 13. BRUCKER *in loc. citat.*). Nor could he have gained this knowledge from any people, of which hiſtory has preſerved any memorials; for we know of none among whom ſcience had made ſuch a progreſs, that a truth ſo remote from common obſervation, and ſo contradictory to the evidence of unimproved ſenſe, would not have been rejected, as it was by all the ſects of Greek philoſophy except the Pythagoreans, who rather revered it as an article of faith, than underſtood it as a diſcovery of ſcience. THRACE was certainly inhabited by a civiliſed nation at ſome remote period; for, when PHILIP of MACEDON opened the gold mines in that country, he found that they had been worked before with great expence and ingenuity, by a people well verſed in mechanics, of whom no memorials whatever were then extant. Of theſe, probably, was ORPHEUS, as well as THAMYRIS, both of whoſe Poems, PLATO ſays, could be read with pleaſure in his time.

† ORPH. Hym. 5.

explain hereafter. Wings are figuratively attributed to him as being the emblems of ſwiftneſs and incubation; by the firſt of which he pervaded matter, and by the ſecond fructified the egg of Chaos. The egg was carried in proceſſion at the celebration of the myſteries, becauſe, as PLUTARCH ſays, it was the material of generation, (ὕλη τῆς γενέσεως*) containing the ſeeds and germs of liſe and motion, without being actually poſſeſſed of either. For this reaſon, it was a very proper ſymbol of Chaos, containing the ſeeds and materials of all things, which, however, were barren and uſeleſs, until the Creator fructified them by the incubation of his vital ſpirit, and releaſed them from the reſtraints of inert matter, by the efforts of his divine ſtrength. The incubation of the vital ſpirit is repreſented on the colonial medals of TYRE, by a ſerpent wreathed round an egg;† for the ſerpent, having the power of caſting his ſkin, and apparently renewing his youth, became the ſymbol of life and vigour, and as ſuch is always made an attendant on the mythological Deities preſiding over health.‡ It is alſo obſerved that animals of the ſerpent kind retain life more pertinaciouſly than any others

---

* Symph. l. 2. † See Plate XVI. Fig. 1. ‡ MACROB. Sat. I. c. 20.

Fig. 7
Fig. 1
COL TY RO METR
Fig. 2
Fig. 3
Fig. 4
ΒΑΣΙΛΙΣΣΑΣ
ΦΙΛΙΣΤΙΔΟΣ
Fig. 5
Fig. 6
ΣΥΡΑΚΟΣΙΩΝ

others except the Polypus, which is ſometimes repreſented upon the Greek Medals,* probably in its ſtead. I have myſelf ſeen the heart of an adder continue its vital motions for many minutes after it has been taken from the body, and even renew them, after it has been cold, upon being moiſtened with warm water, and touched with a ſtimulus.

The Creator, delivering the fructified ſeeds of things from the reſtraints of inert matter by his divine ſtrength, is repreſented on innumerable Greek medals by the Urus, or wild Bull in the act of butting againſt the Egg of Chaos, and breaking it with his horns.† It is true, that the egg is not repreſented with the bull on any of thoſe which I have ſeen; but Mr. D'HANCARVILLE‡ has brought examples from other countries, where the ſame ſyſtem prevailed, which, as well as the general analogy of the Greek

 theology,

---

* See GOLTZ, Tab. II. Fig. 7 & 8.

† See Plate IV. Fig. 1. & Recherches ſur les Arts, Vol. I. Pl. VIII. The Hebrew word *Chroub*, or *Cherub*, ſignified originally, *ſtrong* or *robuſt*; but is uſually employed metaphorically, ſignifying a Bull. See CLERIC. in *Exod.* c. 25.

‡ Recherches ſur les Arts, Lib. I.

theology, proves that the egg muſt have been underſtood, and that the attitude of the bull could have no other meaning. I ſhall alſo have occaſion hereafter to ſhow by other examples, that it was no uncommon practice, in theſe myſtic monuments, to make a part of a groupe repreſent the whole. It was from this horned ſymbol of the power of the Deity, that horns were placed in the portraits of kings, to ſhew that their power was derived from Heaven, and acknowledged no earthly ſuperior. The moderns have indeed changed the meaning of this ſymbol, and given it a ſenſe, of which, perhaps, it would be difficult to find the origin, though I have often wondered that it has never exerciſed the ſagacity of thoſe learned Gentlemen who make Britiſh antiquities the ſubjects of their laborious enquiries. At preſent, it certainly does not bear any character of dignity or power; nor does it ever imply that thoſe, to whom it is attributed, have been particularly favoured by the generative or creative powers.—But this is a ſubject much too important to be diſcuſſed in a digreſſion; I ſhall therefore leave it to thoſe learned Antiquarians, who have done themſelves ſo much honour, and the public ſo much ſervice, by their ſucceſsful enquiries into cuſtoms of of the ſame kind. To their indefatigable induſtry and exquiſite ingenuity I earneſtly recommend it, only obſerving that this modern acceptation of the ſymbol is of conſiderable antiquity, for it is mentioned as proverbial in the Oneirocritics of ARTEMIDORUS ;* and that it is not now confined to GREAT-BRITAIN, but prevails in moſt parts of Chriſtendom, as the ancient acceptation of it did formerly in moſt parts of the world, even among that people from whoſe religion Chriſtianity is derived ; for it is a common mode of expreſſion in the Old Teſtament, to ſay that the horns of any one ſhall be exalted, in order to ſignify that he ſhall be raiſed into power or pre-eminence ; and when MOSES deſcended from the mount with the ſpirit of God ſtill upon him, his head appeared horned.†

To the head of the bull was ſometimes joined the organ of generation, which repreſented not only the ſtrength of the Creator, but the peculiar direction of

* Lib. I. c. 12.

† *Exod.* c. XXXIV. v. 35. Ed. vulgat. Other tranſlators underſtood the expreſſion metaphorically, and ſuppoſe it to mean radiated, or luminous.

of it to the moſt beneficial purpoſe, the propagation of ſenſitive beings. Of this there is a ſmall bronze in the Muſeum of Mr. TOWNLEY, of which an engraving is given in Plate III. Fig. I.*

Sometimes this generative attribute is repreſented by the ſymbol of the Goat, ſuppoſed to be the moſt ſalacious of animals, and therefore adopted upon the ſame principles as the bull and the ſerpent.† The choral odes, ſung in honour of the generator BACCHUS, were hence called τραγωδιαι, or ſongs of the goat; a title which is now applied to the dramatic dialogues anciently inſerted in theſe odes, to break their uniformity. On a medal, ſtruck in honour of AUGUSTUS, the goat terminates in the tail of a fiſh, to ſhow the generative power incorporated with water. Under his feet is the globe of the earth, ſuppoſed to be fertiliſed by this union; and upon his back, the cornucopia, repreſenting the reſult of this fertility.‡

---

* See the tail-piece to Sir W. H.'s Letter.

† Του δε τραγου απεθεωταν (ὁι Αιγυπτιοι) καθαπερ και παρα τοις Ελλησι τετιμησθαι λεγουσι τον Πριαπου, δια το γεννητικον μοριον. DIODOR. Lib. I. p. 78.

‡ Plate IX. Fig. 13.

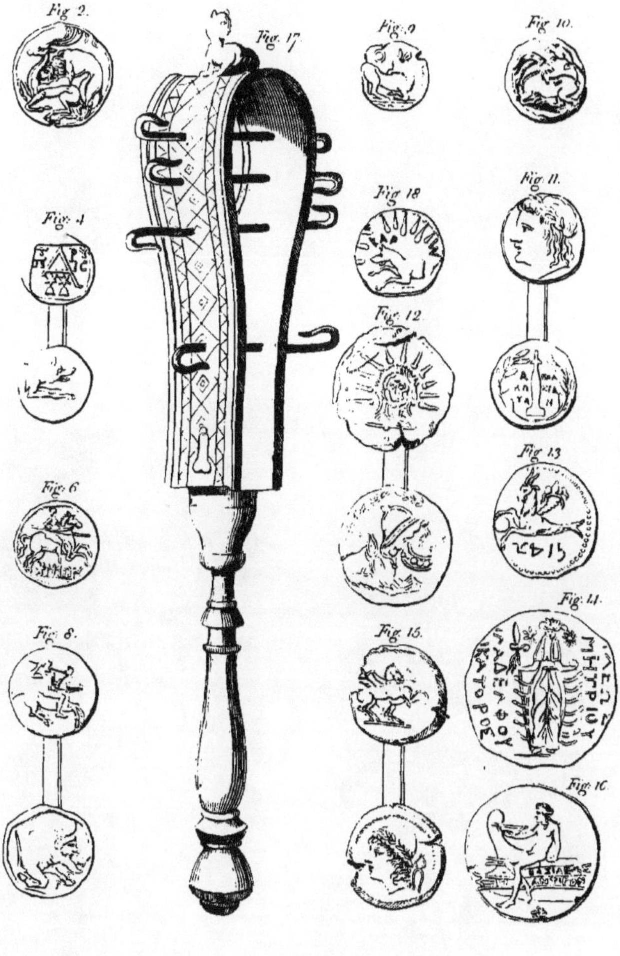
Fig. 2.
Fig. 17
Fig. 9
Fig. 10.
Fig. 18
Fig. 11.
Fig. 4
Fig. 12
Fig. 6
Fig. 13
Fig. 8.
Fig. 15.
Fig. 14.
Fig. 16.

Mr. D'Hancarville attributes the origin of all these ſymbols to the ambiguity of words; the ſame term being employed in the primitive language to ſignify God and a Bull, the Univerſe and a Goat, Life and a Serpent. But words are only the types and ſymbols of ideas, and therefore muſt be poſterior to them, in the ſame manner as ideas are to their objects. The words of a primitive language, being imitative of the ideas from which they ſprung, and of the objects they meant to expreſs, as far as the imperfections of the organs of ſpeech will admit, there muſt neceſſarily be the ſame kind of analogy between them, as between the ideas and objects themſelves. It is impoſſible, therefore, that in ſuch a language any ambiguity of this ſort could exiſt, as it does in ſecondary languages; the words of which, being collected from various ſources, and blended together without having any natural connexion, become arbitrary ſigns of convention, inſtead of imitative repreſentations of ideas. In this caſe it often happens, that words, ſimilar in ſorm, but different in meaning, have been adopted from different ſources, which, being blended together, loſe their little difference of form, and retain their entire difference of meaning. Hence ambiguities

ariſe,

arife, fuch as thofe above mentioned, which could not poffibly exift in an original tongue.

The Greek poets and artifts frequently give the perfonification of a particular attribute for the Deity himfelf; hence he is called Ταυροβοας, Ταυρωπος, Ταυρομορφος,* &c. and hence the initials and monograms of the Orphic epithets applied to the Creator, are found with the bull, and other fymbols, on the Greek medals.† It muft not be imagined from hence, that the ancients fuppofed the Deity to exift under the form of a bull, a goat, or a ferpent: on the contrary, he is always defcribed in the Orphic theology, as a general pervading Spirit, without form, or diftinct locality of any kind; and appears, by a curious fragment preferved by PROCLUS,‡ to have been no other than attraction perfonified. The felf-created mind (νοος αυτογενεθλος) of the eternal

---

* ORPH. *Hymn.* v. et xxix.

† Numm. Vet. Pop. et Urb. Tab. XXXIX. Fig. 19 et 20. They are on moft of the Medals of Marfeilles, Naples, Thurium, and many other cities.

‡ In *Tim.* III. et *Frag. Orphic.* Ed. Gefner.

eternal Father is ſaid to have ſpread the heavy bond of love through all things (πασιν ενεπηξεν δεσμον περιβριθη Ερωτος), in order that they might endure for ever. This eternal Father is Κρονος, time or eternity, perſonified; and ſo taken for the unknown Being that fills eternity and infinity. The ancient Theologiſts knew that we could form no poſitive idea of infinity, whether of power, ſpace, or time; it being fleeting and fugitive, and eluding the underſtanding by a continued and boundleſs progreſſion. The only notion we have of it is from the addition or diviſion of finite things, which ſuggeſt the idea of infinite, only from a power we feel in ourſelves of ſtill multiplying and dividing without end. The Schoolmen indeed were bolder, and, by a ſummary mode of reaſoning, in which they were very expert, proved that they had as clear and adequate an idea of infinity, as of any finite ſubſtance whatever. Infinity, ſaid they, is that which has no bounds.— This negation, being a poſitive aſſertion, muſt be founded on a poſitive idea. We have therefore a poſitive idea of infinity.

The Eclectic Jews, and their followers, the Ammonian and Chriſtian Platonics, who endeavoured to make their own philoſophy and religion conform to the ancient theology, held infinity of ſpace to be only the immenſity of the divine preſence. Ὁ Θεος ἑαυτου τοπος ἐστι* was their dogma, which is now inſerted into the Confeſſional of the Greek Church†. This infinity was diſtinguiſhed by them from common ſpace, as time was from eternity. Whatever is eternal or infinite, ſaid they, muſt be abſolutely indiviſible; becauſe diviſion is in itſelf inconſiſtent with infinite continuity and duration: therefore ſpace and time are diſtinct from infinity and eternity, which are void of all parts and gradations whatever. Time is meaſured by years, days, hours, &c. and diſtinguiſhed by paſt, preſent, and future; but theſe, being diviſions, are excluded from eternity, as locality is from infinity, and as both are from the Being who fills both; who can therefore feel no ſucceſſion of events, nor know any gradation of diſtance; but muſt comprehend infinite duration as if it were one moment, and infinite extent as if it were but a ſingle point‡. Hence the Ammonian Platonics ſpeak of him

---

* PHILO. *de Leg. Alleg.* Lib. I. JO. DAMASC. *de Orth. Fid.*

† MOSHEIM. Nota in Sect. xxiv. CUDW. *Syſt. Intellect.*

‡ See BOETH. *de Conſol. Philoſ.* Lib. IV. Proſ. 6.

him as concentered in his own unity, and extended through all things, but participated of by none. Being of a nature more refined and elevated than intelligence itſelf, he could not be known by ſenſe, perception, or reaſon; and being the cauſe of all, he muſt be anterior to all, even to eternity itſelf, if conſidered as eternity of time, and not as the intellectual unity, which is the Deity himſelf, by whoſe emanations all things exiſt, and to whoſe proximity or diſtances they owe their degrees of excellence or baſeneſs. *Being* itſelf, in its moſt abſtract ſenſe, is derived from him; for that which is the cauſe and beginning of all *Being*, cannot be a part of that *All* which ſprung from himſelf: therefore he is not *Being*, nor is *Being* his *Attribute*; for that which has an attribute, cannot have the abſtract ſimplicity of pure unity. All *Being* is in its nature finite; for, if it was otherwiſe, it muſt be without bounds every way; and therefore could have no gradation of proximity to the firſt cauſes, or conſequent pre-eminence of one part over another: for, as all diſtinctions of time are excluded from infinite duration, and all diviſions of locality from infinite extent, ſo are all degrees of priority from infinite progreſſion. The mind *is* and *acts* in itſelf; but the abſtract unity of the firſt cauſe is neither in itſelf, nor in another ;—not in itſelf, becauſe that would imply modification, from which abſtract ſimplicity is neceſſarily exempt ; nor in another, becauſe then there would be an hypoſtatical duality, inſtead of abſolute unity. In both caſes there would be a locality of hypoſtaſis, inconſiſtent with intellectual infinity. As all phyſical attributes were excluded from this metaphyſical abſtraction, which they called their firſt cauſe, he muſt of courſe be deſtitute of all moral ones, which are only generaliſed modes of action of the former. Even ſimple abſtract truth was denied him; for truth, as PROCLUS ſays, is merely the relative to falſhood ; and no relative can exiſt without a poſitive or correlative. The Deity therefore who has no falſhood, can have no truth, in our ſenſe of the word.*

As metaphyſical theology is a ſtudy very generally, and very deſervedly neglected at preſent, I thought this little ſpecimen of it might be entertaining, from its

* PROCLUS *in Theolog. Platon.* Lib. I. et II.

its novelty, to most readers; especially as it is intimately connected with the ancient system, which I have here undertaken to examine. Those, who wish to know more of it, may consult PROCLUS on the Theology of PLATO, where they will find the most exquisite ingenuity most wantonly wasted. No persons ever showed greater acuteness or strength of reasoning than the Platonics and Scholastics; but having quitted common sense, and attempted to mount into the intellectual world, they expended it all in abortive efforts, which may amuse the imagination, but cannot satisfy the understanding.

The ancient Theologists showed more discretion; for, finding that they could conceive no idea of infinity, they were content to revere the Infinite Being in the most general and efficient exertion of his power, attraction; whose agency is perceptible through all matter, and to which all motion may, perhaps, be ultimately traced. This power, being personified, became the secondary Deity, to whom all adoration and worship were directed, and who is therefore frequently considered as the sole and supreme cause of all things. His agency being supposed to extend through the whole material world,

and

and to produce all the various revolutions by which its ſyſtem is ſuſtained, his attributes were of courſe extremely numerous and varied. Theſe were expreſſed by various titles and epithets in the myſtic hymns and litanies, which the artiſts endeavoured to repreſent by various forms and characters of men and animals. The great characteriſtic attribute was repreſented by the Organ of Generation in that ſtate of tenſion and rigidity which is neceſſary to the due performance of its functions. Many ſmall images of this kind have been found among the ruins of HERCULANEUM and POMPEII, attached to the bracelets, which the chaſte and pious matrons of antiquity wore round their necks and arms. In theſe, the organ of generation appears alone, or only accompanied with the Wings of Incubation,* in order to ſhow that the devout wearer devoted herſelf wholly and ſolely to procreation, the great end for which ſhe was ordained. So expreſſive a ſymbol, being conſtantly in her view, muſt keep her attention fixed on its natural object, and continually remind her of the gratitude ſhe owed the Creator, for having taken her into his ſervice, made

* Plate II. Fig. 2. engraved from one in the Britiſh Muſeum.

made her a partaker of his moſt valuable bleſſings, and employed her as the paſſive inſtrument in the exertion of his moſt beneficial power.

The Female Organs of Generation were revered* as ſymbols of the generative powers of Nature or matter, as the male were of the generative powers of God. They are uſually repreſented emblematically, by the Shell, or *Concha Veneris*, which was therefore worn by devout perſons of antiquity, as it ſtill continues to be by pilgrims, and many of the common women of ITALY. The union of both was expreſſed by the hand mentioned in Sir WILLIAM HAMILTON's Letter ;† which, being a leſs explicit ſymbol, has eſcaped the attention of the Reformers, and is ſtill worn, as well as the ſhell, by the women of ITALY, though without being underſtood. It repreſented the act of generation, which was conſidered as a ſolemn ſacrament, in honour of the Creator, as will be more fully ſhown hereafter.

The

* AUGUST. *de Civ. Dei.* Lib. VI. c. 9.

† See Plate II. Fig. I. from one in the Britiſh Muſeum, in which both ſymbols are united.

The Male Organs of Generation are ſometimes found repreſented by ſigns of the ſame ſort, which might properly be called the ſymbols of ſymbols. One of the moſt remarkable of theſe is a croſs, in the form of the letter T,* which thus ſerved as the emblem of creation and generation, before the Church adopted it as the ſign of ſalvation; a lucky coincidence of ideas, which, without doubt, facilitated the reception of it among the Faithful. To the repreſentative of the male organs was ſometimes added a Human Head, which gives it the exact appearance of a crucifix; as it has on a medal of CYZICUM, publiſhed by M. PELLERIN.† On an ancient medal, found in CYPRUS, which, from the ſtyle of workmanſhip, is certainly anterior to the Macedonian conqueſt, it appears with the chapelet or roſary, ſuch as is now uſed in the Romiſh churches;‡ the beads of which were uſed, anciently, to reckon time.§ Their being placed

---

* Recherches ſur les Arts, Lib. I. c. 3.

† See Plate VIII. Fig. 2.

‡ Plate VIII. Fig. 3. from PELLERIN. Similar medals are in the HUNTER collection, and are evidently of Phœnician Work.

§ Recherches ſur les Arts, Lib. I. c. 3.

Fig. 1

Fig. 2.

Fig. 3.

placed in a circle, marked its progreſſive continuity; while their ſeparation from each other marked the diviſions, by which it is made to return on itſelf, and thus produce years, months, and days. The ſymbol of the creative power is placed upon them, becauſe theſe diviſions were particularly under his influence and protection; the Sun being his viſible image, and the centre of his power, from which his emanations extended through the univerſe. Hence the Egyptians, in their ſacred hymns, called upon Osiris, as the being who dwelt concealed in the embraces of the Sun;* and hence the great luminary itſelf is called Κοσμοκρατωρ (Ruler of the World) in the Orphic Hymns.†

This general emanation of the pervading ſpirit of God, by which all things are generated and maintained, is beautifully deſcribed by Virgil, in the following lines:

Deum namque ire per omnes
Terraſque, tractuſque maris, cœlumque profundum.
Hinc pecudes, armenta, viros, genus omne ferarum,
Quemque ſibi tenues naſcentem arceſſere vitas.
Scilicet huc reddi deinde, ac reſoluta referri
Omnia: nec morti eſſe locum, ſed viva volare
Sideris in numerum, atque alto ſuccedere cœlo.‡

---

* Plutarch. *de Iſid. & Oſir.*

† See Hymn VII.

‡ Georgic. Lib. IV. Ver. 221.

The Etherial Spirit is here deſcribed as expanding itſelf through the univerſe, and giving life and motion to the inhabitants of earth, water, and air, by a participation of his own eſſence, each particle of which returned to its native ſource, at the diſſolution of the body which it animated. Hence, not only men, but all animals, and even vegetables, were ſuppoſed to be impregnated with ſome particles of the divine nature infuſed into them, from which their various qualities and diſpoſitions, as well as their powers of propagation, were ſuppoſed to be derived. Theſe appeared to be ſo many emanations of the divine attributes, operating in different modes and degrees, according to the nature of the beings to which they belonged. Hence, the characteriſtic properties of animals and plants were not only regarded as repreſentations, but as actual emanations of the Divine Power, conſubſtantial with his own eſſence.* For this reaſon, the ſymbols were treated with greater reſpect and veneration than if they had been merely ſigns and characters of convention. PLUTARCH ſays, that moſt of the Egyptian Prieſts held

---

* PROCLUS *in Theol. Plat.* Lib. I. p. 56 & 57.

the bull Apis, who was worſhipped with ſo much ceremony, to be only an image of the ſpirit of Osiris.* This I take to have been the real meaning of all the animal worſhip of the Egyptians, about which ſo much has been written, and ſo little diſcovered. Thoſe animals or plants, in which any particular attribute of the Deity ſeemed to predominate, became the ſymbols of that attribute, and were accordingly worſhipped as the images of Divine Providence, acting in that particular direction. Like many other cuſtoms, both of ancient and modern worſhip, the practice, probably, continued long after the reaſons upon which it was founded were either wholly loſt, or only partially preſerved, in vague traditions. This was the caſe in Egypt; for, though many of the Prieſts knew or conjectured the origin of the worſhip of the Bull, they could give no rational account why the Crocodile, the Ichneumon, and the Ibis, received ſimilar honours. The ſymbolical characters, called hieroglyphics, continued to be eſteemed by them, as more holy and venerable than the conventional repreſentations of

 ſounds,

* *De Iſ. & Oſ.*

ſounds, notwithſtanding their manifeſt inferiority; yet it does not appear, from any accounts extant, that they were able to aſſign any reaſon for this preference. On the contrary, STRABO tells us, that the Egyptians of his time were wholly ignorant of their ancient learning and religion,* though impoſtors continually pretended to explain it. Their ignorance in theſe points is not to be wondered at, conſidering that the moſt ancient Egyptians, of whom we have any authentic accounts, lived after the ſubverſion of their monarchy, and deſtruction of their temples by the Perſians, who uſed every endeavour to annihilate their religion; firſt, by command of CAMBYSES,† and then of OCHUS.‡ What they were, before this calamity, we have no direct information; for HERODOTUS is the earlieſt traveller, and he viſited this country when in ruins.

It is obſervable in all modern religions, that men are ſuperſtitious in proportion as they are ignorant, and that thoſe, who know leaſt of the principles of religion, are the moſt earneſt and fervent in the practice

* Lib. XVII. † HERODOT. Lib. III. STRABO, Lib. XVII.
‡ PLUTARCH. *de Iſ. & Oſ.*

practice of its exteriour rites and ceremonies. We may suppose from analogy, that this was the case with the Egyptians. The learned and rational merely respected and revered the sacred animals, whilst the vulgar worshipped and adored them. The greatest part of the former being, as is natural to suppose, destroyed by the persecution of the Persians, this worship and adoration became general; different cities adopting different animals as their tutelar Deities, in the same manner as the Catholics now put themselves under the protection of different Saints and Martyrs. Like them too, in the fervency of their devotion for the imaginary agent, they forgot the original cause.

The custom of keeping sacred animals as images of the divine attributes, seems once to have prevailed in GREECE as well as EGYPT; for the God of Health was represented by a living Serpent at EPIDAURUS, even in the last stage of their religion.* In general, however, they preferred wrought images; not

* LIV. *Hist. Epitom.* Lib. XI.

not from their superiority in art, which they did not acquire till after the time of HOMER,* when their theology was entirely corrupted; but because they had thus the means of expressing their ideas more fully, by combining several forms together, and showing, not only the divine attribute, but the mode and purpose of its operation. For instance; the celebrated bronze in the VATICAN has the male organs of generation placed upon the head of a Cock, the emblem of the Sun, supported by the neck and shoulders of a Man. In this composition they represented the generative power of the Ερως, the OSIRIS, MITHRAS, or BACCHUS, whose center is the sun, incarnate with man. By the inscription on the pedestal, the attribute, thus personified, is styled *The Saviour of the World*, (Σωτηρ κοσμου); a title always venerable, under whatever image it be represented.†

The Egyptians showed this incarnation of the Deity by a less permanent, though equally expressive

* When HOMER praises any Work of art, he calls it the work of Sidonians.

† See Plate II. Fig. 3.

preſſive ſymbol. At MENDES a living Goat was kept as the image of the generative power, to whom the Women preſented themſelves naked, and had the honour of being publickly enjoyed by him. HERODOTUS ſaw the act openly performed (ες επιδειξιν ανθρωπων,) and calls it a prodigy (τερας). But the Egyptians had no ſuch horror of it; for it was to them a repreſentation of the incarnation of the Deity, and the communication of his creative ſpirit to man. It was one of the ſacraments of that ancient Church, and was, without doubt, beheld with that pious awe and reverence with which devout perſons always contemplate the myſteries of their faith, whatever they happen to be; for, as the learned and orthodox Biſhop WARBURTON, whoſe authority it is not for me to diſpute, ſays, *from the nature of any action morality cannot ariſe, nor from its effects:** therefore, for aught we can tell, this ceremony, however ſhocking it may appear to modern manners and opinions, might have been intrinſically meritorious at the time of its celebration, and afforded a truly edifying ſpectacle to the Saints of ancient EGYPT. Indeed,

* Div. Leg. Book I. c. 4.

Indeed, the Greeks do not ſeem to have felt much horror or diſguſt at the imitative repreſentation of it, whatever the Hiſtorian might have thought proper to expreſs at the real celebration. Several ſpecimens of their ſculpture in this way have eſcaped the fury of the Reformers, and remained for the inſtruction of later times. One of theſe, found among the ruins of HERCULANEUM, and kept concealed in the Royal Muſeum at PORTICI, is well known. Another exiſts in the collection of Mr. TOWNLEY, which I have thought proper to have engraved for the benefit of the learned.* It may be remarked, that in theſe monuments the Goat is *paſſive* inſtead of *active*; and that the *human ſymbol* is repreſented as incarnate with the *divine*, inſtead of the *divine* with the *human*: but this is in fact no difference; for the Creator, being of both ſexes, is repreſented indifferently of either. In the other ſymbol of the Bull, the ſex is equally varied; the Greek Medals having ſometimes a Bull, and ſometimes a Cow,† which, STRABO tells us, was

* Plate VII. the tail-piece to this diſcourſe.

† See Plate IV. Fig. 1, 2, 3. and Plate III. Fig. 4. engraved from medals belonging to me.

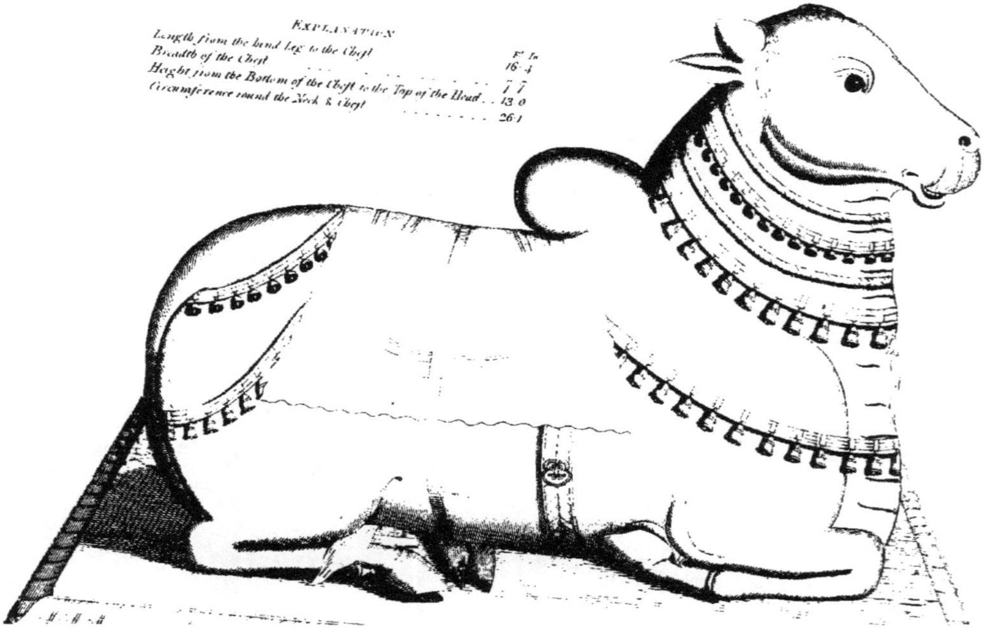

EXPLANATION

	Ft	In
Length from the hind Leg to the Chest	16	4
Breadth of the Chest	7	7
Height from the Bottom of the Chest to the Top of the Head	13	0
Circumference round the Neck & Chest	26	1

was employed as the ſymbol of VENUS, the paſſive generative power at MOMEMPHIS, in EGYPT.* Both the Bull and the Cow are alſo worſhipped at preſent by the Hindoos, as ſymbols of the male and female, or generative and nutritive powers of the Deity. The Cow is in almoſt all their Pagodas; but the Bull is revered with ſuperior ſolemnity and devotion. At TANJOUR is a monument of their piety to him, which even the inflexible perſeverance, and habitual induſtry of the natives of that country, could ſcarcely have erected, without greater knowledge in practical mechanics than they now poſſeſs. It is a ſtatue of a Bull lying down, hewn, with great accuracy, out of a ſingle piece of hard granite, which has been conveyed by land from the diſtance of a hundred miles, although its weight, in its preſent reduced ſtate, muſt be at leaſt a hundred tons.† The Greeks ſometimes made their Taurine BACCHUS, or Bull, with a human face, to expreſs both ſexes, which they ſignified by the initial of the epithet Διφυης,

* Lib. XVII.

† See Plate XVII. with the meaſurements, as made by Capt. PATTERSON on the ſpot.

placed under him.* Over him they frequently put the radiated asterisc, which represents the Sun, to show the Deity, whose attribute he was intended to express.† Hence we may perceive the reason why the Germans, who, according to CÆSAR,‡ worshipped the Sun, carried a brazen Bull, as the image of their God, when they invaded the Roman dominions in the time of MARIUS;§ and even the chosen People of Providence, when they made unto themselves an image of the God who was to conduct them through the desert, and cast out the ungodly from before them, made it in the shape of a young Bull, or Calf.||

The Greeks, as they advanced in the cultivation of the imitative arts, gradually changed the animal for

* See Plate IV. Fig. 2. from a medal of Naples in the HUNTER Collection.

† See Plate IV. Fig. 2. and Plate XV. Fig. 6. from a medal of Cales, belonging to me.

‡ *De B. G.* Lib. VI.

§ PLUT. *in Mario.*

|| *Exod.* c. 32. with PATRICK's *Commentary.*

for the human form, preſerving ſtill the original character. The Human Head was at firſt added to the Body of the Bull;* but afterwards the whole figure was made human, with ſome of the features, and general character of the animal, blended with it.† Oftentimes, however, theſe mixed figures had a peculiar and proper meaning, like that of the Vatican Bronze; and were not intended as mere refinements of art. Such are the Fawns and Satyrs, who repreſent the emanations of the Creator, incarnate with man, acting as his angels and miniſters in the work of univerſal generation. In copulation with the Goat, they repreſent the reciprocal incarnation of man with the Deity, when incorporated with univerſal matter: for the Deity, being both male and female, was both active and paſſive in procreation; firſt animating man by an emanation from his own eſſence, and then employing that emanation to reproduce, in conjunction with the common productive powers of Nature, which are no other than his own prolific ſpirit transfuſed through matter.

 Theſe

* See the Medals of Naples, Gela, &c. Plate IV. Fig. 2. and Plate IX. Fig. 8. are ſpecimens; but the Coins are in all Collections.

† See *Bronzi d'Herculano*, Tom. V. Plate 5.

These mixed beings are derived from PAN, the principle of universal order; of whose personified image they partake. PAN is addressed in the Orphic Litanies, as the first-begotten Love, or Creator incorporated in universal matter, and so forming the world.* The heaven, the earth, water, and fire, are said to be members of him; and he is described as the origin and source of all things, (παντοφυης γενετωρ. παντων) as representing matter animated by the Divine Spirit. Lycæan PAN was the most ancient and revered God of the Arcadians,† the most ancient people of GREECE. The epithet LYCÆAN, (Λυκαιος) is usually derived from λυκος, a Wolf; though it is impossible to find any relation which this etymology can have with the Deities to which it is applied; for the epithet Λυκαιος, or Λυκειος, (which is only the different pronunciation of a different dialect) is occasionally applied to almost all the Gods. I have therefore no doubt, but that it ought to be derived from the old word λύκος or λυκη, light; from which came the Latin word *lux*.

---

* Hymn. x.

† DIONYS. *Antiq. Rom.* Lib. I. c. 32.

*lux.** In this ſenſe it is a very proper epithet for the divine nature, of whoſe eſſence light was ſuppoſed to be. I am confirmed in this conjecture by a word in the *Electra* of Sophocles, which ſeems hitherto to have been miſunderſtood. At the opening of the play, the old tutor of Orestes, entering Argos with his young Pupil, points out to him the moſt celebrated public buildings, and amongſt them the Lycæan Forum, τυ λυκοκτονυ Θεu, which the ſcholiaſt and tranſlators interpret, *of the Wolf-killing God*, though there is no reaſon whatever why this epithet ſhould be applied to Apollo. But, if we derive the compound from λυκος, light, and εκτεινειν, to extend, inſtead of κτεινειν, to kill, the meaning will be perfectly juſt and natural; for *light-extending* is of all others the propereſt epithet for the Sun. Sophocles, as well as Virgil, is known to have been an admirer of ancient expreſſions, and to have imitated Homer more than any other Attic Poet; therefore, his employing an obſolete word is not to be wondered at. Taking this etymology as the true one, the Lycæan Pan of Arcadia is Pan *the luminous*; that is, the divine eſſence of light incorporated

* Macrob. *Sat.* XVII.

corporated in univerſal matter. The Arcadians called him τον της ὑλης Κυριον, the Lord of Matter, as MACROBIUS rightly tranſlates it.* He was hence called SYLVANUS by the Latins; *Sylva* being, in the ancient Pelaſgian and Æolian Greek, from which the Latin is derived, the ſame as ὑλη; for it is well known to all who have compared the two languages attentively, that the *Sigma* and *Vau* are letters, the one of which was partially, and the other generally omitted by the Greeks, in the refinement of their pronunciation and orthography, which took place after the emigration of the Latian and Etruſcan Colonies. The Chorus in the *Ajax* of SOPHOCLES addreſs PAN by the title of Ἁλιπλαγκτος,† probably becauſe he was worſhipped on the Shores of the ſea; water being reckoned the beſt and moſt prolific of the ſubordinate elements,‡ upon which the ſpirit of God, according to MOSES, or the plaſtic Nature, according to the Platonics, operating, produced life and motion on earth. Hence the Ocean is ſaid by HOMER to be the ſource of

* Sat. I. c. 22. † Ver. 703.

‡ PINDAR. *Olymp.* I. ver. 1. DIODOR. Sic. Lib. I. p. 11.

of all things;* and hence the use of water in baptism, which was to regenerate, and, in a manner, new create the person baptised; for the soul, supposed by many of the primitive Christians to be naturally mortal, was then supposed to become immortal.† Upon the same principle, the figure of PAN, engraved in Plate V. Fig. I.‡ is represented pouring water upon the Organ of Generation; that is, invigorating the active creative power by the prolific element upon which it acted; for water was considered as the essence of the passive principle, as fire was of the active; the one being of terrestrial, and the other of ætherial origin. Hence, St. JOHN the Baptist, who might have acquired some knowledge of the ancient theology, through its revivers, the Eclectic Jews, says: *I, indeed, baptise you in Water to repentance; but he that cometh after me, who is more powerful than I am, shall baptise you in the Holy Spirit, and in Fire*:§ that is, I only purify and refresh the soul, by a communion with the terrestrial principle of life; but he that cometh after me, will regenerate and restore it, by a

communion

---

* IL. ξ. ver. 246. & φ ver. 196.

† CLEMENTINA, *Hom.* XII. ARNOB. *adv. Gentes,* Lib. II.

‡ See tail-piece to the Italian Letter. The original is among the antiquities found in HERCULANEUM, now in the Museum of PORTICI.

§ *Matth.* c. 3.

communion with the etherial principle*. Pan is again addreſſed in the Salaminian Chorus of the ſame Tragedy of Sophocles, by the titles of Author and Director of the Dances of the Gods (Θεων χοροποι' αναξ) as being the author and diſpoſer of the regular motions of the univerſe, of which theſe divine dances were ſymbols, which are ſaid in the ſame paſſage to be (αυτοδαη) *ſelf-taught* to him. Both the Gnoſſian and Nyſian dances are here included,† the former ſacred to Jupiter, and the latter to Bacchus; for Pan, being the principle of univerſal order, partook of the nature of all the other Gods. They were perſonifications of particular modes of acting of the great all-ruling principle; and he, of his general law and pre-eſtabliſhed harmony by which he governs the univerſe. Hence he is often repreſented playing on a pipe; muſic being the natural emblem of this phyſical harmony. According to Plutarch, the Jupiter Ammon of the Africans

---

* It is the avowed intention of the learned and excellent work of Grotius, to prove that there is nothing new in Chriſtianity. What I have here adduced, may ſerve to confirm and illuſtrate the diſcoveries of that great and good man. See *de Veritate Relig. Chriſt.* Lib. iv. c. 12.

† Ver. 708.

Africans was the ſame as the PAN of the Greeks.* This explains the reaſon why the Macedonian Kings aſſumed the horns of that God; for, though ALEXANDER pretended to be his ſon, his ſucceſſors never pretended to any ſuch honour; and yet they equally aſſumed the ſymbols, as appears from their medals.† The caſe is, that PAN, or AMMON, being the univerſe, and JUPITER a title of the ſupreme God (as will be ſhown hereafter), the Horns, the emblems of his power, ſeemed the propereſt ſymbols of that ſupreme and univerſal dominion, to which they all, as well as ALEXANDER, had the ambition to aſpire. The figure of AMMON was compounded of the forms of the Ram, as that of PAN was of the Goat; the reaſon of which is difficult to aſcertain, unleſs we ſuppoſe that Goats were unknown in the country where his worſhip aroſe, and that the Ram expreſſed the ſame attribute.‡ In a gem in the Muſeum of

---

* *De Iſ. & Oſ.*

† See Plate IV. Fig. 4. engraved from one of LYSIMACHUS, of exquiſite beauty, belonging to me. ANTIGONUS put the head of PAN upon his Coins, which are not uncommon.

‡ PAUSANIAS (Lib. II.) ſays he knew the meaning of this ſymbol, but did not chuſe to reveal it, it being a part of the Myſtic Worſhip.

Charles Townley, Efq. the Head of the Greek Pan is joined to that of a Ram, on the body of a Cock, over whoſe head is the aſteriſc of the Sun, and below it the head of an aquatic Fowl, attached to the ſame body.* The Cock is the ſymbol of the Sun, probably from proclaiming his approach in the morning; and the aquatic Fowl is the emblem of Water; ſo that this compoſition, apparently ſo whimſical, repreſents the Univerſe between the two great prolific Elements, the one the active, and the other the paſſive cauſe of all things.

The Creator being both male and female, the emanations of his creative ſpirit, operating upon univerſal matter, produced ſubordinate miniſters of both ſexes, and gave, as companions to the Fauns and Satyrs, the Nymphs of the Waters, the Mountains, and the Woods, ſignifying the paſſive productive powers of each, ſubdivided and diffuſed. Of the ſame claſs are the Γενετυλλιδες, mentioned by Pausanias as companions to Venus,† who, as well as Ceres,

* Plate III. Fig. I. † Lib. I.

CERES, JUNO, DIANA, ISIS, &c. was only a perſonification of Nature, or the paſſive principle of Generation, operating in various modes. APULEIUS invokes ISIS by the names of the ELEUSINIAN CERES, CELESTIAL VENUS, and PROSERPINE; and, when the Goddeſs anſwers him, ſhe deſcribes herſelf as follows: "I am," ſays ſhe, "Nature, the Parent "of Things, the Sovereign of the Elements, the Pri-"mary Progeny of Time, the moſt exalted of the "Deities, the firſt of the Heavenly Gods and "Goddeſſes, the Queen of the Shades, the Uni-"form Countenance; who diſpoſe, with my nod, the "luminous heights of heaven, the ſalubrious breezes "of the ſea, and the mournful ſilence of the dead; "whoſe ſingle Deity the whole world venerates, in "many forms, with various rites, and various "names.—The Egyptians, ſkilled in ancient learn-"ing, worſhip me with proper ceremonies, and call "me by my true name, QUEEN ISIS."*

According to the Egyptians, ISIS copulated with her brother OSIRIS in the womb of their mother; from

* *Metamorph.* Lib. XI.

from whence ſprung ARUERIS, or ORUS, the APOLLO of the Greeks.* This allegory means no more than that the active and paſſive powers of Creation united in the womb of Night; where they had been implanted by the unknown Father, Κρονος, or Time, and by their union produced the ſeparation or delivery of the elements from each other; for the name APOLLO is only a title derived from απολυω, *to deliver from*.† They made the robes of ISIS various in their colours and complicated in their folds, becauſe the paſſive, or material power, appeared in various ſhapes and modes, as accommodating itſelf to the active; but the dreſs of OSIRIS was ſimple, and of one luminous colour, to ſhow the unity of his eſſence, and univerſality of his power; equally the ſame through all things.* The luminous, or flame colour, repreſented the Sun, who, in the language of the Theologiſts, was the ſubſtance of his ſacred power, and the viſible image of his intellectual being.* He is called, in the Orphic Litanies, the chain which connects all things together ('ο δ'ανεδραμε δεσμος άπαντων),† as being the principle of attraction; and

---

* PLUTARCH. *de Iſ. & Oſ.* † DAMM. *Lex. Etym.*
†. Hymn. xlvi.

and the Deliverer (λυσιος),* as giving liberty to the innate powers of Nature, and thus fertilising matter. These epithets not only express the theological, but also the physical system of the Orphic School; according to which the Sun, being placed in the centre of the universe, with the Planets moving round, was, by his attractive force, the cause of all union and harmony in the whole; and, by the emanation of his beams, the cause of all motion and activity in the parts. This system is alluded to by HOMER in the allegory of the golden Chain, by which JUPITER suspends all things;† though there is every reason to believe that the Poet himself was ignorant of its meaning, and only related it as he had heard it. The Ammonian Platonics adopted the same system of attraction, but changed its centre from the Sun to their metaphysical Abstraction or incomprehensible Unity, whose emanations pervaded all things, and held all things together.‡

Besides

---

* Hymn. xlix. the Initials of this Epithet are with the Bull on a medal of Naples belonging to me. The Bull has a Human Countenance, and has therefore been called a Minotaur by Antiquarians; notwithstanding he is to be found on different medals, accompanied with all the symbols both of BACCHUS and APOLLO; and with the Initials of most of the Epithets to be found in the Orphic Litanies.

† IL. Θ. Ver. xix.

‡ PROCLUS *in Theol. Plat.* Lib. I. c. 21.

Besides the Fauns, Satyrs, and Nymphs, the incarnate emanations of the active and passive powers of the Creator, we often find in the ancient sculptures certain Androgynous beings possessed of the characteristic organs of both sexes, which I take to represent organised matter in its first stage; that is, immediately after it was released from Chaos, and before it was animated by a participation of the etherial essence of the Creator. In a beautiful gem belonging to R. WILBRAHAM, Esq;* one of these Androgynous figures is represented sleeping, with the Organs of Generation covered, and the Egg of Chaos broken under it. On the other side is BACCHUS the Creator, bearing a Torch, the emblem of etherial fire, and extending it towards the sleeping figure; whilst one of his agents seems only to wait his permission to begin the execution of that office, which, according to every outward and visible sign, he appears able to discharge with energy and effect. The Creator himself leans upon one of those figures commonly called *Sileni*; but which, from their heavy unwieldy forms, were probably intended as personifications

* See Plate V. Fig. 3.

cations of brute inert matter, from which all things are formed, but which, being incapable of producing any thing of itself, is properly represented as the support of the Creative Power, though not actively instrumental in his work. The total baldness of this figure represents the exhausted, unproductive state of matter, when the generative powers were separated from it; for it was an opinion of the ancients, which I remember to have met with in some part of the Works of ARISTOTLE, to which I cannot at present refer, that every act of coition produced a transient chill in the brain, by which some of the roots of the hair were loosened; so that baldness was a mark of sterility acquired by excessive exertion. The figures of PAN have nearly the same forms with that which I have here supposed to represent inert matter; only that they are compounded with those of the Goat, the symbol of the Creative Power, by which matter was fructified and regulated. To this is sometimes added the Organ of Generation, of an enormous magnitude, to signify the application of this power to its noblest end, the procreation of sensitive and rational beings. This composition forms the common PRIAPUS of the Roman Poets, who was worshipped among the other personages of the Heathen Mythology,

Mythology, but underſtood by few of his ancient votaries any better than by the good Women of Isernia. His characteriſtic Organ is ſometimes repreſented by the artiſts in that ſtate of tenſion and rigidity, which it aſſumes when about to diſcharge its functions,* and at other times in that ſtate of tumid languor, which immediately ſucceeds the performance.† In the latter caſe he appears loaded with the productions of Nature, the reſult of thoſe prolific efforts, which in the former caſe he appeared ſo well qualified to exert. I have in Plate V. given a Figure of him in each ſituation, one taken from a bronze in the Royal Muſeum of Portici, and the other from one in that of Charles Townley, Eſq. It may be obſerved, that in the former the muſcles of the face are all ſtrained and contracted, ſo that every nerve ſeems to be in a ſtate of tenſion; whereas in the latter the features are all dilated and fallen, the chin repoſed on the breaſt, and the whole figure expreſſive of languor and fatigue.

If

* Plate V. Fig. 1. from a bronze in the Muſeum at Portici.

† Plate V. Fig. 2. from a bronze in the Muſeum of C. Townley, Eſq.

If the explanation which I have given of these Androgynous figures be the true one, the Fauns and Satyrs, which usually accompany them, must represent abstract emanations, and not incarnations of the Creative Spirit, as when in copulation with the Goat. The Creator himself is frequently represented in a human form; and it is natural that his emanations should partake of the same, though without having any thing really human in their composition. It seems however to have been the opinion in some parts of ASIA, that the Creator was really of a human form. The Jewish Legislator says expressly, that God made Man in his own image, and, prior to the creation of Woman, created him *male and female*,* as he himself consequently was.† Hence an ingenious Author has supposed that these Androgynous figures represented the first individuals of the human race, who, possessing the organs of both sexes, produced children of each. This seems to be the sense in which they were represented by some of the ancient artists: but I have never met with any trace of it in any Greek author, except PHILO the Jew; nor have I

 ever

* Genes. c. i. † PHILO *de Leg. Alleg.* Lib. II.

ever ſeen any monument of ancient art, in which the Bacchus, or Creator in a human form, was repreſented with the generative organs of both ſexes. In the ſymbolical images, the double nature is frequently expreſſed by ſome androgynous inſect, ſuch as the Snail, which is endowed with the organs of both ſexes, and can copulate reciprocally with either: but when the refinement of art adopted the Human Form, it was repreſented by mixing the characters of the male and female bodies in every part, preſerving ſtill the diſtinctive organs of the male. Hence Euripides calls Bacchus θηλυμορφος,* and the Chorus of Bacchanals in the ſame Tragedy addreſs him by maſculine and feminine epithets. † Ovid alſo ſays to him,

—— Tibi, cum ſine cornibus adſtas,
Virgineum caput eſt. ‡

alluding in the firſt line to his Taurine, and in the ſecond to his Androgynous figure.

The ancient Theologiſts were, like the modern, divided into ſects; but, as theſe never diſturbed the peace

* Bacch. V. 358.

† Ω Βρομιε, Βρομιε, Πεδων χθονος ενοσι ποτνια. V. 504.

‡ *Metam.* Lib. IV. V. 18.

peace of ſociety, they have been very little noticed. I have ſollowed what I conceive to be the true Orphic ſyſtem, in the little analyſis which I have here endeavoured to give. This was probably the true Catholic Faith, though it differs conſiderably from another ancient ſyſtem, deſcribed by ARISTOPHANES;* which is more poetical, but leſs philoſophical. According to this, Chaos, Night, Erebus, and Tartarus, were the primitive beings. Night, in the infinite breaſt of Erebus, brought forth an Egg, from which ſprung Love, who mixed all things together; and from thence ſprung the Heaven, the Ocean, the Earth, and the Gods. This ſyſtem is alluded to by the epithet ωογενος, applied to the Creator in one of the Orphic Litanies:† but this could never have been a part of the orthodox faith; for the Creator is uſually repreſented as breaking the Egg of Chaos, and therefore could not have ſprung from it. In the confuſed medley of allegories and traditions contained in the Theogony attributed to HESIOD, Love is placed after Chaos and the Earth, but anterior to every thing elſe. Theſe differences are not to be wondered at; for ARISTOPHANES, ſuppoſing that he underſtood the true ſyſtem, could not with

 ſafety

* Ορνιθ. V. 693. † Hymn. V.

ſafety have revealed it, or even mentioned it any otherwiſe than under the uſual garb of fiction and allegory; and as for the Author of the Theogony, it is evident, from the ſtrange jumble of incoherent fables which he has put together, that he knew very little of it. The ſyſtem alluded to in the Orphic verſes quoted in the *Argonautics*, is in all probability the true one; for it is not only conſiſtent in all its parts, but contains a phyſical truth, which the greateſt of the modern diſcoveries has only confirmed and explained. The others ſeem to have been only poetical corruptions of it, which, extending by degrees, produced that unwieldy ſyſtem of poetical Mythology, which conſtituted the vulgar religion of GREECE.

The Fauns and Satyrs, which accompany the Androgynous figures on the ancient ſculptures, are uſually repreſented as miniſtering to the Creator by exerting their characteriſtic attributes upon them, as well as upon the Nymphs, the paſſive agents of procreation: but what has puzzled the learned in theſe monuments, and ſeems a contradiction to the general ſyſtem of ancient religion, is that many of theſe groupes are in attitudes which are rather adapted to the gratification of diſordered, and unnatural appetites, than to extend procreation.

procreation. But a learned Author, who has thrown infinite light upon these subjects, has effectually cleared them from this suspicion, by showing that they only took the most convenient way to get at the Female Organs of Generation, in those mixed beings who possessed both.* This is confirmed by LUCRETIUS, who asserts, that this attitude is better adapted to the purposes of generation than any other.† We may therefore conclude, that instead of representing them in the act of gratifying any disorderly appetites, the artists meant to show their modesty in not indulging their concupiscence, but in doing their duty in the way best adapted to answer the ends proposed by the Creator.

On the Greek medals, where the Cow is the symbol of the Deity, she is frequently represented licking a Calf, which is sucking her.‡ This is probably meant to show that the Creative Power cherishes and nourishes, as well as generates; for, as all quadrupeds lick

---

* *Recherches sur les Arts*, Liv. I. c. 3.

† Lib. IV. v. 1260.

‡ See Plate IV. Fig. 3. from a medal of DYRRACHIUM, belonging to me.

lick their young, to refreſh and invigorate them immediately after birth, it is natural to ſuppoſe, according to the general ſyſtem of ſymbolical writing, that this action ſhould be taken as an emblem of the effect it was thought to produce. On other medals the Bull or Cow is repreſented licking itſelf;* which, upon the ſame principle, muſt repreſent the ſtrength of the Deity refreſhed and invigorated by the exertion of its own nutritive and plaſtic power upon its own being. On others again is a human head of an Androgynous character, like that of the BACCHUS Διφυης, with the tongue extended over the lower lip, as if to lick ſomething.† This was probably the ſame ſymbol, expreſſed in a leſs explicit manner; it being the common practice of the Greek Artiſts to make a part of a compoſition ſignify the whole, of which I ſhall ſoon have occaſion to give ſome inconteſtable examples. On a Parian medal publiſhed by GOLTZIUS, the Bull licking himſelf is repreſented on one ſide, accompanied

---

* See Plate X. Fig. 2. from one of GORTYNA in the HUNTER Collection; and Plate III. Fig. 4. from one of PARIUM, belonging to me.

† See Plate III. Fig. 4. and Plate X. Fig. 3. from PELLERIN.

accompanied by the asterisc of the Sun, and on the other, the head with the tongue extended, having Serpents, the emblems of life, for hair.* The same medal is in my Collection, except that the serpents are not attached to the head, but placed by it as distinct symbols, and that the animal licking itself is a female accompanied by the initial of the word Θεῦ, instead of the asterisc of the Sun. Antiquarians have called this head a MEDUSA; but, had they examined it attentively on any well-preserved coin, they would have found that the expression of the features means lust, and not rage or horror.† The case is, that Antiquarians have been continually led into error, by seeking for explanations of the devices on the Greek medals in the wild and capricious stories of OVID's *Metamorphoses*, instead of examining the first principles of ancient religion contained in the Orphic Fragments, the writings of PLUTARCH, MACROBIUS, and APULEIUS, and the Choral Odes of the Greek Tragedies. These principles were the subjects of the ancient mysteries, and it is to these that the symbols

on

* GOLTZ. *Insul.* Tab. XIX. Fig. 8.

† See Plate III. Fig. 4.

on the medals always relate; for they were the public acts of the States, and therefore contain the fenfe of nations, and not the caprices of individuals.

As M. D'HANCARVILLE found a complete reprefentation of the Bull breaking the Egg of Chaos in the fculptures of the Japonefe, when only a part of it appears on the Greek monuments; fo we may find in a curious Oriental fragment, lately brought from the facred Caverns of ELEPHANTA, near BOMBAY, a complete reprefentation of the fymbol fo ænigmatically expreffed by the head above mentioned. Thefe Caverns are ancient places of worfhip, hewn in the folid rock with immenfe labour and difficulty. That from which the fragment in queftion was brought, is 130 feet long by 110 wide, adorned with columns and fculptures finifhed in a ftyle very different from that of the Indian Artifts.* It is now neglected; but others of the fame kind are ftill ufed as places of worfhip by the Hindoos, who can give no account of the antiquity of them, which muft neceffarily be very remote, for the Hindoos are a very ancient people;

---

* *Archæol.* Vol. VIII. p. 289.

Fig. 2.

Fig. 4

Fig. 3

and yet the ſculptures repreſent a race of men very unlike them, or any of the preſent inhabitants of INDIA. A ſpecimen of theſe was brought from the Iſland of ELEPHANTA, in the Cumberland man of war, and now belongs to the Muſeum of Mr. TOWNLEY. It contains ſeveral figures, in very high relief; the principal of which are a Man and Woman, in an attitude which I ſhall not venture to deſcribe, but only obſerve, that the action, which I have ſuppoſed to be a ſymbol of refreſhment and invigoration, is mutually applied by both to their reſpective Organs of Generation,* the emblems of the active and paſſive powers of procreation, which mutually cheriſh and invigorate each other.

The Hindoos ſtill repreſent the creative powers of the Deity by theſe ancient ſymbols, the male and female Organs of Generation; and worſhip them with the ſame pious reverence as the Greeks and Egyptians did.† Like them too they have buried the original principles of their Theology under a maſs of poetical Mythology, ſo that few of them can give any more

 perfect

---

* See Plate X. Fig. 1.

† SONNERAT, *Voyage aux Indes*, T. I. p. 180.

perfect account of their faith, than that they mean to worſhip one First Cauſe, to whom the ſubordinate Deities are merely agents, or more properly perſonified modes of action.* This is the doctrine inculcated, and very fully explained in the *Bagvat Geeta*; a moral and metaphyſical work lately tranſlated from the Shanſcrit language, and ſaid to have been written upwards of four thouſand years ago. KRESHNA, or the Deity become incarnate in the ſhape of man, in order to inſtruct all mankind, is introduced, revealing to his diſciples the fundamental principles of true faith, religion, and wiſdom; which are the exact counterpart of the ſyſtem of Emanations, ſo beautifully deſcribed in the lines of VIRGIL before cited. We here find, though in a more myſtic garb, the ſame one principle of life univerſally emanated and expanded, and ever partially returning to be again abſorbed in the infinite abyſs of intellectual being. This reabſorption, which is throughout recommended as the ultimate end of human perfection, can only be obtained by a life of inward meditation and abſtract thought, too ſteady to be interrupted by any

* NIEBUHR, *Voyages*, Vol. II. p. 17.

any worldly incidents, or disturbed by any transitory affections, whether of mind or body. But as such a life is not in the power of any but a Brahman, inferior rewards, consisting of gradual advancements during the transmigrations of the soul, are held out to the soldier, the husbandman, and mechanic, accordingly as they fulfill the duties of their several stations. Even those who serve other Gods, are not excluded from the benefits awarded to every moral virtue; for, as the divine Teacher says, *If they do it with a firm belief, in so doing they involuntarily worship even me. I am he who partaketh of all worship, and I am their reward.** This universal Deity, being the cause of all motion, is alike the cause of Creation, Preservation, and Destruction; which three attributes are all expressed in the mystic syllable *om.* To repeat this in silence, with firm devotion, and immoveable attention, is the surest means of perfection,† and consequent reabsorption, since it leads to the contemplation of the Deity, in his three great characteristic attributes.

* *Bagvat Geeta*, p. 81. † Ibid. p. 74.

The firſt and greateſt of theſe, the creative or generative attribute, ſeems to have been originally repreſented by the union of the male and female Organs of Generation, which, under the title of the *Lingam*, ſtill occupies the central and moſt interior receſſes of their temples or pagodas; and is alſo worn, attached to bracelets, round their necks and arms.* In a little portable Temple brought from the ROHILLA country during the late war, and now in the Britiſh Muſeum, this compoſition appears mounted on a pedeſtal, in the midſt of a ſquare area, ſunk in a block of white alabaſter.† Round the pedeſtal is a Serpent, the emblem of life, with his head reſted upon his tail, to denote eternity, or the conſtant return of time upon itſelf, whilſt it flows through perpetual duration, in regular revolutions, and ſtated periods. From under the body of the ſerpent ſprings the Lotus or Water Lily, the Nelumbo of LINNÆUS, which overſpreads the whole of the area not occupied by the figures at the corners. This plant grows in the water, and, amongſt

---

* SONNERAT, *Voyage aux Indes*, Liv. II. p. 180. Planche LIV.

† See Plate XI.

Plate XV
Fig. 1
Fig. 2
Fig. 3
Fig. 13
Fig. 4.
Fig. 5.
Fig. 6
Fig. 7
Fig. 8.
Fig. 9.
Fig. 10
Fig. 11
Fig. 12

amongſt its broad leaves, puts forth a flower, in the centre of which is formed the ſeed-veſſel, ſhaped like a bell or inverted cone, and punctuated on the top with little cavities or cells, in which the ſeeds grow.* The orifices of theſe cells being too ſmall to let the ſeeds drop out when ripe, they ſhoot forth into new plants, in the places where they were formed; the bulb of the veſſel ſerving as a matrice to nouriſh them, until they acquire ſuch a degree of magnitude as to burſt it open, and releaſe themſelves; after which, like other aquatic weeds, they take root wherever the current depoſits them. This plant therefore, being thus productive of itſelf, and vegetating from its own matrice, without being foſtered in the earth, was naturally adopted as the ſymbol of the productive power of the waters, upon which the active ſpirit of the Creator operated in giving life and vegetation to matter. We accordingly find it employed in every part of the northern hemiſphere, where the Symbolical Religion, improperly called Idolatry, does or ever did prevail. The ſacred images of the Tartars, Japoneſe, and Indians, are

* See Plate XV. Fig. 5.

are almoſt all placed upon it; of which numerous inſtances occur in the publications of KÆMPFER, CHAPPE D'AUTEROCHE, and SONNERAT. The upper part of the baſe of the *Lingam* alſo conſiſts of this flower, blended and compoſed with the female Organ of Generation, which it ſupports: and the ancient author of the *Bagvat Geeta* ſpeaks of the Creator BRAHMA, as ſitting upon his Lotus throne.* The figures of ISIS upon the Iſiac table, hold the ſtem of this plant, ſurmounted by the ſeed-veſſel in one hand, and the croſs,† repreſenting the male Organs of Generation, in the other; thus ſignifying the univerſal power, both active and paſſive, attributed to that Goddeſs. On the ſame Iſiac table is alſo the repreſentation of an Egyptian temple, the columns of which are exactly like the plant which ISIS holds in her hand, except that the ſtem is made larger, in order to give it that ſtability which is neceſſary to ſupport a roof and entablature.‡ Columns and capitals of the ſame kind are ſtill exiſting, in great numbers, among the ruins of THEBES,

* P. 91. † See Plate XV. Fig. 3. from PIGNORIUS.

‡ See Plate XV. Fig. 1. from PIGNORIUS.

THEBES, in EGYPT; and more particularly upon thoſe very curious ones in the Iſland of PHILÆ, on the borders of ETHIOPIA, which are, probably, the moſt ancient monuments of art now extant; at leaſt, if we except the neighbouring temples of THEBES. Both were certainly built when that city was the ſeat of wealth and empire, which it was, even to a proverb, during the Trojan war.* How long it had then been ſo, we can form no conjecture; but that it ſoon after declined, there can be little doubt; for, when the Greeks, in the reign of PSAMMETICUS, (generally computed to have been about 530 years after the Siege of TROY) firſt became perſonally acquainted with the interior parts of that country, MEMPHIS had been for many ages its capital, and THEBES was in a manner deſerted. HOMER makes ACHILLES ſpeak of its immenſe wealth and grandeur, as a matter generally known and acknowledged; ſo that it muſt have been of long eſtabliſhed fame, even in that remote age. We may therefore fairly conclude, that the greateſt part of the ſuperb edifices now remaining, were executed, or at leaſt begun,

* HOM. *Iliad*. I. Ver. 381.

begun, before that time; many of them being ſuch as could not have been finiſhed, but in a long term of years, even if we ſuppoſe the wealth and power of the ancient Kings of EGYPT to have equalled that of the greateſt of the Roman Emperors. The finiſhing of TRAJAN's column, in three years, has been juſtly thought a very extraordinary effort; for there muſt have been, at leaſt, three hundred good ſculptors employed upon it: and yet, in the neighbourhood of THEBES, we find whole temples of enormous magnitude, covered with figures carved in the hard and brittle granite of the Libyan mountains, inſtead of the ſoft marbles of PAROS and CARRARA. Travellers, who have viſited that country, have given us but imperfect accounts of the manner in which they are finiſhed; but, if one may judge by thoſe upon the Obeliſc of RAMESES, now lying in fragments at ROME, they are infinitely more laboured than thoſe of TRAJAN's Column. An eminent Sculptor, with whom I examined that Obeliſc, was decidedly of opinion, that they muſt have been finiſhed in the manner of Gems, with a graving tool; it appearing impoſſible for a chiſel to cut red granite with ſo much neatneſs and preciſion. The age of RAMESES is uncertain; but the generality of modern Chronologers

ſuppoſe

ſuppoſe that he was the ſame perſon as SESOSTRIS, and reigned at THEBES about 1500 years before the Chriſtian Æra, and about 300 before the Siege of TROY. Their dates are however merely conjectural, when applied to events of this remote antiquity. The Egyptian Prieſts of the Auguſtan Age had a tradition, which they pretended to confirm by records, written in Hieroglyphics, that their Country had once poſſeſt the dominion of all ASIA and ÆTHIOPIA, which their King RAMSES, or RAMESES, had conquered.* Though this account may be exaggerated, there can be no doubt, from the buildings ſtill remaining, but that they were once at the head of a great Empire; for all hiſtorians agree that they abhorred navigation, had no ſea-port, and never enjoyed the benefits of foreign commerce, without which, EGYPT could have no means of acquiring a ſufficient quantity of ſuperfluous wealth to erect ſuch expenſive monuments, unleſs from tributary provinces; eſpecially if all the lower part of it was an uncultivated bog, as HERODOTUS, with great appearance of probability, tells us it anciently was. Yet HOMER, who appears to have

* TACIT. *Ann.* Lib. II. c. 60.

known all that could be known in his age, and transfmitted to pofterity all he knew, feems to have heard nothing of their empire or conquefts. Thefe were obliterated and forgotten by the rife of new Empires; but the renown of their ancient wealth ftill continued, and afforded a familiar object of comparifon, as that of the MOGUL does at this day, though he is become one of the pooreft Sovereigns in the world.

But far as thefe Egyptian remains lead us into unknown ages, the fymbols they contain appear not to have been invented in that country, but to have been copied from thofe of fome other people, ftill anterior, who dwelt on the other fide of the Erythræan Ocean. One of the moft obvious of them is the hooded Snake, which is a reptile peculiar to the fouth-eaftern parts of ASIA, but which I found reprefented, with great accuracy, upon the obelifc of RAMESES, and have alfo obferved frequently repeated on the Ifiac Table, and other fymbolical works of the Egyptians. It is alfo diftinguifhable among the Sculptures in the Sacred Caverns of the Ifland of ELEPHANTA;* and appears

* NIEBUHR, *Voyage*, Vol. II.

appears frequently added, as a characteristic symbol, to many of the Idols of the modern Hindoos, whose absurd tales concerning its meaning are related at length by M. SONNERAT; but they are not worth repeating. Probably we should be able to trace the connexion through many more instances, could we obtain accurate drawings of the ruins of Upper EGYPT.

By comparing the Columns which the Egyptians formed in imitation of the Nelumbo Plant, with each other, and observing their different modes of decorating them, we may discover the origin of that order of architecture which the Greeks called Corinthian, from the place of its supposed invention. We first find the plain Bell, or Seed-vessel, used as a Capital, without any further alteration than being a little expanded at bottom, to give it stability.* In the next instance, the same Seed-vessel is surrounded by the leaves of some other Plant; † which is varied

* See Plate XV. Fig. 8. from NORDEN.

† See Plate XV. Fig. 9. from NORDEN.

in different Capitals according to the different meanings intended to be expressed by these additional symbols. The Greeks decorated it in the same manner, with the leaves of the Acanthus, and other sorts of foliage; whilst various other symbols of their religion were introduced as ornaments on the entablature, instead of being carved upon the walls of the cell, or shafts of the columns. One of these, which occurs most frequently, is that which the Architects call the Honey-suckle, but which, as Sir JOSEPH BANKS (to whom I am indebted for all that I have said concerning the Lotus) clearly shewed me, must be meant for the young shoots of this Plant, viewed horizontally, just when they have burst the Seed-vessel, and are upon the point of falling out of it. The ornament is variously composed on different buildings; it being the practice of the Greeks to make vegetable, as well as animal monsters, by combining different symbolical Plants together, and blending them into one; whence they are often extremely difficult to be discovered. But the specimen I have given, is so strongly characterised, that it cannot easily be mistaken.* It appears on many Greek

* Plate XV. Fig. 4. from the Ionian Antiquities. Ch. II. Pl. xii.

Greek medals with the animal ſymbols, and perſonified attributes of the Deity; which firſt led me to imagine that it was not a mere ornament, but had ſome myſtic meaning, as almoſt every decoration employed upon their ſacred edifices indiſputably had.

The ſquare area, over which the Lotus is ſpread, in the Indian monument before mentioned, was occaſionally floated with water; which, by means of a forcing machine, was firſt thrown in a ſpout upon the *Lingam*. The pouring of water upon the ſacred ſymbols, is a mode of worſhip very much practiſed by the Hindoos, particularly in their devotions to the Bull and the *Lingam*. Its meaning has been already explained, in the inſtance of the Greek figure of Pan, repreſented in the act of paying the ſame kind of worſhip to the ſymbol of his own procreative power.* The areas of the Greek temples were, in like manner, in ſome inſtances, floated with water; of which I ſhall ſoon give an example. We alſo find, not unfrequently, little portable

* See Plate V. Fig. 1.

portable temples, nearly of the ſame form, and of Greek workmanſhip; the areas of which were equally floated by means of a fountain in the middle, and which, by the figures in relief that adorn the ſides, appear evidently to have been dedicated to the ſame worſhip of PRIAPUS, or the *Lingam*.* The ſquare area is likewiſe impreſſed upon many ancient Greek medals, ſometimes divided into four, and ſometimes into a greater number of compartments.† Antiquarians have ſuppoſed this to be merely the impreſſion of ſomething put under the coin, to make it receive the ſtroke of the die more ſteadily; but, beſides that it is very ill adapted to this purpoſe, we find many coins which appear, evidently, to have received the ſtroke of the hammer (for ſtriking with a balance is of late date) on the ſide marked with this ſquare. But what puts the queſtion out of all doubt, is, that impreſſions of exactly the ſame kind are found upon the

* See Plate XII. Fig. 12. from one in the Collection of Mr. TOWNLEY.

† See Plate XII. Fig. 1. from one of SELINUS, and Fig. 3. from one of SYRACUSE, belonging to me.

Fig. 1
Fig. 2
Fig. 4
Fig. 5
Fig. 6
Fig. 7
Fig. 8
Fig. 12
Fig. 10
Fig. 11

the little Talifmans, or myftic paftes, taken out of the Egyptian Mummies, which have no impreffion whatever on the reverfe.* On a little brafs medal of SYRACUSE, we alfo find the afterifc of the Sun placed in the centre of the fquare, in the fame manner as the *Lingam* is on the Indian monument.† Why this quadrangular form was adopted, in preference to any other, we have no means of difcovering, from any known Greek or Egyptian fculptures; but from this little Indian temple, we find that the four corners were adapted to four of the fubordinate Deities, or perfonified modes of action of the great univerfal Generator, reprefented by the fymbol in the middle, to which the others are reprefented as paying their adorations, with geftures of humility and refpect.‡

What is the precife meaning of thefe four fymbolical figures, it is fcarcely poffible for us to difcover,

* See Plate XII. Fig. 2. from one in the Collection of Mr. TOWNLEY.

† See Plate XII. Fig. 3. The medal is extremely common, and the quadrangular impreffion is obfervable upon a great number of the more ancient Greek medals, generally with fome fymbol of the Deity in the centre. See thofe of ATHENS, LYTTUS, MARONEA, &c.

‡ See Plate XI.

cover, from the ſmall fragments of the myſtic learning of the ancients, which are now extant. That they were however intended as perſonified attributes, we can have no doubt; for we are taught by the venerable authority of the *Bagvat Geeta*, that all the ſubordinate Deities were ſuch, or elſe canoniſed Men, which theſe figures evidently are not. As for the mythological tales now current in INDIA, they throw the ſame degree of light upon the ſubject, as OVID's Metamorphoſes do on the ancient Theology of GREECE; that is, juſt enough to bewilder and perplex thoſe who give up their attention to it. The ancient Author before cited is deſerving of more credit; but he has ſaid very little upon the ſymbolical worſhip. His work, nevertheleſs, clearly proves that its principles were preciſely the ſame as thoſe of the Greeks and Egyptians, among whoſe remains of art or literature, we may, perhaps, find ſome probable analogies to aid conjecture. The Elephant is, however, a new ſymbol in the weſt; the Greeks never having ſeen one of thoſe animals before the expedition of ALEXANDER,* although the uſe

* PAUSAN. Lib. I. c. 12.

uſe of ivory was familiar among them even in the days of HOMER. Upon this Indian monument the head of the Elephant is placed upon the body of a Man with four hands, two of which are held up as prepared to ſtrike with the inſtruments they hold, and the other two pointed down as in adoration of the *Lingam*. This figure is called GONNIS and POLLEAR by the modern Hindoos; but neither of theſe names is to be found in the *Geeta*, where the Deity only ſays, *that the learned behold him alike in the reverend Brahman perfected in knowledge, in the Ox, and in the Elephant*. What peculiar attributes the Elephant was meant to expreſs, the ancient Writer has not told us; but, as the characteriſtic properties of this animal are ſtrength and ſagacity, we may conclude that his image was intended to repreſent ideas ſomewhat ſimilar to thoſe which the Greeks repreſented by that of MINERVA, who was worſhipped as the Goddeſs of Force and Wiſdom, of War and Counſel. The Indian GONNIS is indeed male, and MINERVA female; but this difference of ſexes, however important it may be in phyſical, is of very little conſequence in metaphyſical beings, MINERVA being, like the other Greek deities, either male, or female, both.* On the Medals of the PTOLEMIES, under whom the Indian ſymbols became familiar to the Greeks through the commerce of ALEXANDRIA, we find her repeatedly repreſented with the Elephant's ſkin upon her head, inſtead of a helmet; and with a countenance between male and female, ſuch as the artiſt would naturally give her, when he endeavoured to blend the Greek and Indian ſymbols, and mould them into one.† MINERVA is ſaid by the Greek Mythologiſts to have been born without a Mother, from the head of JUPITER, who was delivered of her by the aſſiſtance of VULCAN. This, in plain language, means no more than that ſhe was a pure emanation of the Divine Mind, operating by means of the univerſal agent Fire, and not, like others of the allegorical perſonages, ſprung from any of the particular operations of the Deity upon external matter. Hence ſhe is ſaid to be next in dignity to her Father, and to be endowed with all his attributes;‡ for, as wiſdom is the moſt exalted quality of the

---

* Αρσεν και θηλυς εφυς. ORPH. εις Αθην.

† See Plate XII. Fig. 5. engraved from one belonging to me.

‡ HOR. Lib. I. Od. 12. CALLIMACH. εις Αθην.

the mind, and the Divine Mind the perfection of wiſdom, all its attributes are the attributes of Wiſdom, under whoſe direction its power is always exerted. Strength and Wiſdom therefore, when conſidered as attributes of the Deity, are in fact one and the ſame. The Greek MINERVA is uſually repreſented with the ſpear uplifted in her hand, in the ſame manner as the Indian GONNIS holds the battle-axe.* Both are given to denote the deſtroying power equally belonging to Divine Wiſdom, as the creative or preſerving. The ſtatue of JUPITER at LABRANDA in CARIA held in his hand the battle-axe, inſtead of thunder; and on the medals of TENEDOS and THYATIRA, we find it repreſented alone as the ſymbol of the Deity, in the ſame manner as the thunder is upon a great variety of other medals. *I am the thunderbolt*, ſays the Deity in the *Bagvat Geeta*;† and when we find this ſuppoſed engine of Divine vengeance upon the medals, we muſt not imagine that it is meant for the weapon of the Supreme God, but for the ſymbol of his deſtroying attribute.

What

* See Plate XII. Fig. 11. from a medal of SELEUCUS I. belonging to me.

† P. 86.

What inſtrument the GONNIS holds in his other hand, is not eaſily aſcertained, it being a little injured by the carriage. In one of thoſe pointed downwards he holds the Lotus flower, to denote that he has the direction of the paſſive powers of production; and in the other, a golden Ring or Diſc, which, I ſhall ſoon ſhew, was the ſymbol by which many nations of the Eaſt repreſented the Sun. His head is drawn into a conical, or pyramidal form, and ſurrounded by an ornament which evidently repreſents Flames; the Indians, as well as the Greeks, looking upon fire as the eſſence of all active power; whence perpetual lamps are kept burning in the Holy of Holies of all the great Pagodas in India, as they were anciently in the Temple of JUPITER AMMON, and many others both Greek and Barbarian;* and the incarnate God in the *Bagvat Geeta* ſays, *I am the Fire reſiding in the bodies of all things which have life.*† Upon the forehead of the GONNIS is a creſcent repreſenting the the Moon, whoſe power over the waters of the Ocean cauſed her to be regarded as the ſovereign of the great

* See PLUT. *de Orac. defect.*

† P. 113.

great nutritive Element, and whofe mild rays, being accompanied by the refrefhing dews, and cooling breezes of the night, made her naturally appear to the inhabitants of hot countries as the comforter and reftorer of the earth. *I am the Moon* (fays the Deity in the Bagvat Geeta) *whofe nature it is to give the quality of tafte and relifh, and to cherifh the herbs and plants of the field.** The light of the Sun, Moon and Fire, were however all but one, and equally emanations of the Supreme Being. *Know*, fays the Deity in the fame ancient dialogue, *that the light which proceedeth from the Sun, and illuminateth the world, and the light which is in the Moon, and in the Fire, are mine. I pervade all things in Nature, and guard them with my beams.*† In the figure now under confideration a kind of pre-eminence feems to be given to the Moon over the Sun; proceeding probably from the Hindoos not poffeffing the true Solar Syftem, which muft however have been known to the people from whom they learnt to calculate eclipfes, which they ftill continue to do, though upon principles not underftood by themfelves. They now place the earth

* P. 113. † Ibid.

earth in the centre of the univerſe, as the later Greeks did, among whom we alſo find the ſame preference given to the Lunar ſymbol; JUPITER being repreſented, on a medal of ANTIOCHUS VIII. with the Creſcent upon his head, and the aſteriſc of the Sun in his hand.* In a paſſage of the *Bagvat Geeta* already cited we find the Elephant and Bull mentioned together as ſymbols of the ſame kind; and on a medal of SELEUCUS NICATOR we find them united by the horns of the one being placed on the head of the other.† The later Greeks alſo ſometimes employed the Elephant as the univerſal ſymbol of the Deity; in which ſenſe he is repreſented on a medal of ANTIOCHUS VI. bearing the Torch, the emblem of the univerſal agent Fire, in his proboſcis, and the Cornucopia, the reſult of its exertion, in his tail.‡

On another corner of the little Indian Pagoda, is a figure with four heads, all of the ſame pointed form

---

* Plate XII. Fig. 10. from one belonging to me.

† See Plate XII. Fig. 9. and GESNER, *Num. Reg. Syr.* Tab. VIII. Fig. 23.

‡ See Plate XII. Fig. 8. and GESNER, *Num. Reg. Syr.* Tab. VIII. Fig. 1.

form as that of the GONNIS. This I take to represent BRAHMA, to whom the Hindoos attribute four mouths, and say that with them he dictated the four Beads, or Veads, the mystic volumes of their religion.* The four Heads are turned different ways, but exactly resemble each other. The Beards have been painted black, and are sharp and pointed, like those of Goats, which the Greeks gave to PAN, and his subordinate emanations, the Fauns and Satyrs. Hence I am inclined to believe, that the BRAHMA of the Indians is the same as the PAN of the Greeks; that is, the Creative Spirit of the Deity transfused through matter, and acting in the four elements represented by the four heads. The Indians indeed admit of a fifth element, as the Greeks did likewise; but this is never classed with the rest, being of an ætherial, and more exalted nature, and belonging peculiarly to the Deity. *Some call it Heaven, some Light, and some Æther*, says PLUTARCH.† The Hindoos now call it *Occus*, by which they seem to mean pure ætherial Light or Fire.

This

* *Bagvat Geeta*, Note 41. † Ει Apud DELPH.

This mode of repreſenting the allegorical perſonages of Religion with many heads and limbs to expreſs their various attributes, and extenſive operation, is now univerſal in the Eaſt,* and ſeems anciently not to have been unknown to the Greeks, at leaſt if we may judge by the epithets uſed by PINDAR and other early Poets.† The union of two ſymbolical heads is common among the ſpecimens of their art now extant, as may be ſeen upon the medals of SYRACUSE, MARSEILLES, and many other cities. Upon a gem of this ſort in the collection of Mr. TOWNLEY, the ſame ideas which are expreſſed on the Indian pagoda by the diſtinct figures BRAHMA and GONNIS, are expreſſed by the united heads of AMMON and MINERVA. AMMON, as before obſerved, was the PAN of the Greeks, and MINERVA is here evidently the ſame as the GONNIS, being repreſented after the Indian manner, with the Elephant's ſkin on her head, inſtead of an helmet.‡ Both theſe heads appear ſeparate upon different medals of the PTOLEMIES,§ under

* See KÆMPFER, CHAPPE D'AUTEROCHE, SONNERAT, &c.

† Such as ἑκατογκεφαλος, ἑκατονταπαρανος, ἑκατογχειρος, &c.

‡ See Plate XII. Fig. 7.

§ See Plate XII. Fig. 5 and 6.

under one of whom this gem was probably engraved, ALEXANDRIA having been for a long time the great centre of religions, as well as of trade and ſcience.

Next to the figure of BRAHMA on the Pagoda is the Cow of Plenty, or the ſemale emblem of the generative or nutritive power of the Earth; and at the other corner, next to the GONNIS, is the figure of a Woman with a head of the ſame conic or pyramidal form, and upon the front of it a flame of Fire, from which hangs a Creſcent.* This ſeems to be the female perſonification of the Divine Attributes repreſented by the GONNIS or POLLEAR; for the Hindoos, like the Greeks, worſhip the Deity under both ſexes, though they do not attempt to unite both in one figure. *I am the Father and the Mother of the world*, ſays the incarnate God in the *Bagvat Geeta*.† *Amongſt cattle*, adds he in a ſubſequent part, *I am the Cow* KAMADHOOK. *I am the prolific* KANDARP, *the God of Love*.‡ Theſe two ſentences, by being placed together, ſeem to imply ſome relation between this *God of Love*, and the *Cow Kamadhook*; and, were we to read the

O words

* See Plate XI. † P. 80. ‡ P. 86.

words without punctuation, as they are in all ancient orthography, we ſhould think the Author placed the God of Love amongſt the Cattle; which he would naturally do, if it were the cuſtom of his religion to repreſent him by an animal ſymbol. Among the Egyptians, as before obſerved, the Cow was the ſymbol of VENUS, the Goddeſs of Love, and paſſive generative power of Nature. On the capitals of one of the temples of PHILÆ we ſtill find the heads of this Goddeſs repreſented of a mixed form; the horns and ears of the Cow being joined to the beautiful features of a Woman in the prime of life;* ſuch as the Greeks attributed to that VENUS, whom they worſhipped as the Mother of the prolific God of Love, CUPID, who was the perſonification of animal deſire or concupiſcence, as the Orphic Love, the Father of Gods and Men, was of univerſal attraction. The Greeks, who repreſented the Mother under the form of a beautiful Woman, naturally repreſented the Son under the form of a beautiful Boy; but a people who repreſented the Mother under the form of a Cow, would as naturally repreſent the Son under the form of

* See Plate XV. Fig. 10.

of a Calf. This ſeems to be the caſe with the Hindoos, as well as with the Egyptians; wherefore KANDARP may be very properly placed among the Cattle.

By following this analogy we may come to the true meaning of a much-celebrated object of devotion, recorded by another ancient Writer, of a more venerable character. When the Iſraelites grew clamorous on account of the abſence of MOSES, and called upon AARON to make them a God to go before them, he ſet up a golden Calf; to which the people ſacrificed, and feaſted; and then roſe up (as the Tranſlator ſays) *to play:* but in the original the term is more ſpecific, and means, in its plain direct ſenſe, that particular ſort of play which requires the concurrence of both ſexes,* and which was therefore a very proper concluſion of a ſacrifice to CUPID, though highly diſpleaſing to the God who had brought them out of EGYPT. The Egyptian Mythologiſts, who appear to have invented this ſecondary Deity of Love, were probably the inventors likewiſe

---

* *Exod.* C. 32.

of a ſecondary PRIAPUS, who was the perſonification of that particular generative faculty, which ſprings from animal deſire, as the primary PRIAPUS was of the great generative principle of the Univerſe. Hence, in the allegories of the Poets, this Deity is ſaid to be a ſon of BACCHUS and VENUS; that is, the reſult of the active and paſſive generative powers of Nature. The ſtory of his being the ſon of a Grecian Conqueror, and born at LAMPSACUS, ſeems to be a corruption of this allegory.

Of all the nations of antiquity the Perſians were the moſt ſimple and direct in the worſhip of the Creator. They were the Puritans of the Heathen World, and not only rejected all images of God or his Agents, but alſo temples and altars, according to HERODOTUS,* whoſe authority I prefer to any other, becauſe he had an opportunity of converſing with them before they had adopted any foreign ſuperſtitions.† As they worſhipped the ætherial Fire without any medium of perſonification or allegory, they

* Lib. I.

† HYDE, ANGUETIL, and other modern Writers, have given us the operoſe ſuperſtitions of the preſent Parſees for the ſimple theiſm of the ancient Perſians.

they thought it unworthy of the dignity of the God, to be repreſented by any definite form, or circumſcribed to any particular place. The Univerſe was his temple, and the all-pervading element of Fire his only ſymbol. The Greeks appear originally to have held ſimilar opinions; for they were long without ſtatues;* and PAUSANIAS ſpeaks of a Temple at SICYON, built by ADRASTUS,† who lived an age before the Trojan war; which conſiſted of columns only, without wall or roof, like the Celtic temples of our Northern Anceſtors, or the Pyrætheia of the Perſians, which were circles of ſtones, in the centre of which was kindled the ſacred Fire,‡ the ſymbol of the God. HOMER frequently ſpeaks of places of worſhip conſiſting of an area and altar only, (τεμενος βωμος τε) which were probably incloſures like theſe of the Perſians, with an altar in the centre. The temples dedicated to the Creator BACCHUS, which the Greek Architects called *hypæthral*, ſeem to have been anciently of the ſame kind; whence probably came the title περικιονιος (*ſurrounded*

* PAUSAN. Lib. VII. and IX.

† Lib. II.

‡ STRAB. Lib. XV.

rounded with columns) attributed to that God in the Orphic Litanies.* The remains of one of these are ſtill extant at PUZZUOLI near NAPLES, which the inhabitants call the Temple of SERAPIS : but the ornaments of Grapes, Vaſes, &c. found among the ruins, prove it to have been of BACCHUS'S. SERAPIS was indeed the ſame Deity worſhipped under another form, being equally a perſonification of the Sun.† The architecture is of the Roman times ; but the ground plan is probably that of a very ancient one, which this was made to replace ; for it exactly reſembles that of a Celtic temple in ZEELAND, publiſhed in STUKELEY'S *Itinerary*.‡ The ranges of ſquare buildings which incloſe it are not properly parts of the temple, but apartments of the Prieſts, places for victims and ſacred utenſils ; and chapels dedicated to ſubordinate Deities introduced by a more complicated and corrupt worſhip, and probably unknown to the founders of the original edifice.§ The portico, which runs parallel with theſe buildings,‖ incloſed the *Temenos*, or area of ſacred

* Hymn. 46.

† DIODOR. SIC. Lib. I. MACROB. *Sat.* Lib. I. C. 20.

‡ See Plate XIII. Fig. 1 and 2, and Plate XII. Fig. 4.

§ Plate XIII. Fig. 2. *a—a.*

‖ Plate XIII. Fig. 2. *b—b.*

Fig 1

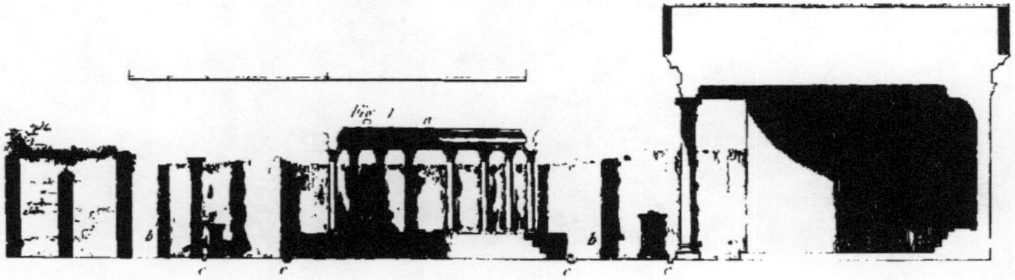

Fig 3

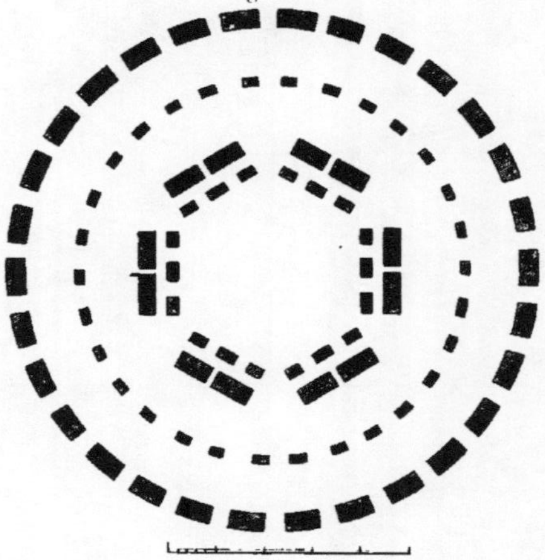

Fig 2

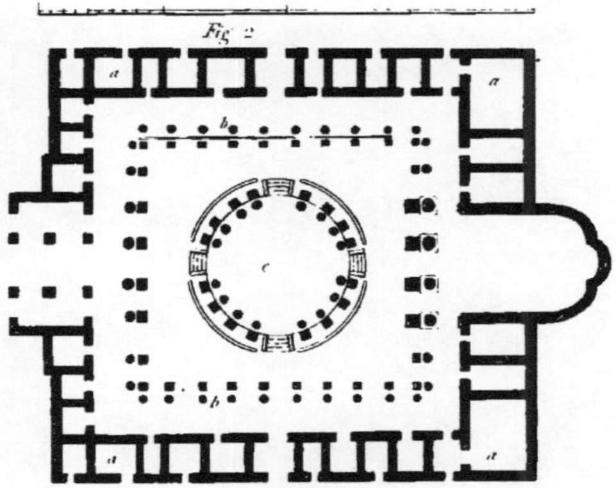

ſacred ground, which in the *Pyrætheia* of the Perſians was circular, but is here quadrangular, as in the Celtic Temple in ZEELAND, and the Indian Pagoda before deſcribed. In the centre was the Holy of Holies, the Seat of the God, conſiſting of a circle of columns raiſed upon a baſement, without roof or walls, in the middle of which was probably the ſacred Fire, or ſome other ſymbol of the Deity.* The ſquare area in which it ſtood, was ſunk below the natural level of the ground,† and, like that of the little Indian Pagoda, appears to have been occaſionally floated with water, the drains and conduits being ſtill to be ſeen,‡ as alſo ſeveral fragments of ſculpture repreſenting waves, ſerpents, and various aquatic animals, which once adorned the baſement.§ The BACCHUS περικιονιος here worſhipped, was, as we learn from the Orphic Hymn above cited, the Sun in his character of Extinguiſher of the Fires which once pervaded the Earth. This he was ſuppoſed to have

* See Plate XIII. Fig. 1. *a*, and Fig. 2. *c*.

† See Plate XIII. Fig. 1. *b—b*.

‡ See Plate XIII. Fig. 1. *c—c*.

§ See Plate XIV. Fig. 2.

have done by exhaling the waters of the Ocean, and ſcattering them over the land, which was thus ſuppoſed to have acquired its proper temperature and fertility. For this reaſon the Sacred Fire, the eſſential image of the God, was ſurrounded by the element which was principally employed in giving effect to the beneficial exertions of his great attribute.

Theſe Orphic Temples were, without doubt, emblems of that fundamental principle of the myſtic faith of the Ancients, the Solar Syſtem; Fire, the eſſence of the Deity, occupying the place of the Sun, and the columns ſurrounding it as the ſubordinate parts of the Univerſe. Remains of the worſhip of Fire continued among the Greeks even to the laſt, as appears from the Sacred Fires kept in the interior apartment, or Holy of Holies, of almoſt all their temples, and places of worſhip: and, though the Ammonian Platonics, the laſt profeſſors of the ancient religion, endeavoured to conceive ſomething beyond the reach of ſenſe and perception, as the eſſence of their Supreme God; yet, when they wanted to illuſtrate and explain the modes of action of this metaphyſical Abſtraction, who was more ſubtile than

Intelligence

Intelligence itſelf, they do it by images and compariſons of Light and Fire.*

From a paſſage of HECATÆUS, preſerved by DIODORUS SICULUS, I think it is evident that STONEHENGE, and all the other monuments of the ſame kind found in the North, belonged to the ſame religion, which appears, at ſome remote period, to have prevailed over the whole Northern Hemiſphere. According to that ancient Hiſtorian, *the Hyperboreans inhabited an Iſland beyond* GAUL, *as large as* SICILY, *in which* APOLLO *was worſhipped in a circular Temple conſiderable for its ſize and riches.*† APOLLO, we know, in the language of the Greeks of that age, can mean no other than the Sun, which, according to CÆSAR, was worſhipped by the Germans, when they knew of no other Deities except Fire and the Moon.‡ The Iſland I think can be no other than BRITAIN, which at that time was only known to the Greeks by the vague

P reports

* See PROCLUS *in Theol. Platon.* Lib. I. c. 19.

† Νηον αξιολογον, αναθημασι πολλοις κεκοσμημενον, σφαιροειδη τῳ σχηματι. DIOD. SIC. Lib. II.

‡ *De B. Gal.* Lib. VI.

reports of Phœnician Mariners, ſo uncertain and obſcure, that HERODOTUS, the moſt inquiſitive and credulous of Hiſtorians, doubts of its exiſtence.* The circular Temple of the Sun being noticed in ſuch ſlight and imperfect accounts, proves that it muſt have been ſomething ſingular and important; for, if it had been an inconſiderable ſtructure, it would not have been mentioned at all; and, if there had been many ſuch in the country, the Hiſtorian would not have employed the ſingular number. STONHENGE has certainly been a circular Temple, nearly the ſame as that already deſcribed of the BACCHUS περικιονιος at PUZZUOLI, except that in the latter the nice execution, and beautiful ſymmetry of the parts, are in every reſpect the reverſe of the rude but majeſtic ſimplicity of the former; in the original deſign they differ but in the form of the Area.† It may therefore be reaſonably

* Lib. III. c. 15.

† See Plate XIII. Fig. 2 and 3. I have preferred WEBB's Plan of STONEHENGE to STUKELEY's and SMITH's, after comparing each with the ruins now exiſting. They differ materially only in the Cell, which WEBB ſuppoſes to have been a Hexagon, and STUKELEY a Section of an Ellipſis. The poſition of the Altar is merely conjectural; wherefore I have

ſonably ſuppoſed, that we have ſtill the ruins of the identical Temple deſcribed by HECATÆUS, who, being an Aſiatic Greek, might have received his information from ſome Phœnician Merchant, who had viſited the interior parts of BRITAIN when trading there for Tin. MACROBIUS mentions a Temple of the ſame kind and form upon MOUNT ZILMISSUS in THRACE, dedicated to the Sun under the title of BACCHUS SEBAZIUS.* The large Obeliſcs of ſtone found in many parts of the North, ſuch as thoſe at RUDSTONE,† and near BURROUGHBRIDGE in YORKSHIRE,‡ belong to the ſame religion; obeliſcs being, as PLINY obſerves, ſacred to the Sun, whoſe rays they repreſented both by their form and name.§ An ancient Medal of APOLLONIA in ILLYRIA, belonging to the Muſeum of the late Dr. HUNTER, has the head of APOLLO

 crowned

have omitted it; and I much doubt whether either be right in their Plans of the Cell, which ſeems, as in other Druidical Temples, to have been meant for a Circle, but incorrectly executed.

* *Sat.* Lib. I. c. 18.

† *Archæologia*, Vol. V.

‡ Now called the Devil's Arrows. See STUKELEY's *Itin.* Vol. I. Tab. 90.

§ *Hiſt. Nat.* Lib. xxxvi. Sec. 14.

crowned with Laurel on one ſide, and on the other an Obeliſc terminating in a croſs, the leaſt explicit repreſentation of the Male Organs of Generation.* This has exactly the appearance of one of thoſe croſſes, which were erected in church-yards and croſs roads for the adoration of devout perſons, when devotion was more prevalent than at preſent. Many of theſe were undoubtedly erected before the eſtabliſhment of Chriſtianity, and converted, together with their Worſhippers, to the true Faith. Anciently they repreſented the generative power of Light, the eſſence of God; *for God is Light, and never but in unapproached Light dwelt from Eternity*, ſays MILTON, who in this, as well as many other inſtances, has followed the Ammonian Platonics, who were both the reſtorers and corrupters of the ancient theology. They reſtored it from the maſs of poetical mythology, under which it was buried, but refined and ſublimated it with abſtract metaphyſics, which ſoared as far above human reaſon as the poetical mythology ſunk below it. From the ancient Solar Obeliſcs came the Spires and Pinnacles with which our Churches are

† Plate IX. Fig. 11. and *Nummi Pop. & Urb.* Tab. X. Fig. 7.

ſtill decorated, ſo many ages after their myſtic meaning has been forgotten. Happily for the beauty of theſe edifices, it was forgotten; otherwiſe the Reformers of the laſt century would have deſtroyed them, as they did the Croſſes and Images; for they might with equal propriety have been pronounced heatheniſh and prophane.

As the Obeliſc was the ſymbol of Light, ſo was the Pyramid of Fire, deemed to be eſſentially the ſame. The Egyptians, among whom theſe forms are the moſt frequent, held that there were two oppoſite powers in the world, perpetually acting contrary to each other; the one creating, and the other deſtroying: the former they called Osiris, and the latter Typhon.* By the contention of theſe two, that mixture of good and evil, which, according to ſome verſes of Euripides quoted by Plutarch,† conſtituted the harmony of the world, was ſuppoſed to be produced. This opinion of the neceſſary mixture of good and evil was, according to Plutarch, of

* Plutarch. *de Iſ. & Oſ.*

† *De Iſ. & Oſ.* p. 455. Ed. Reiſkii.

of immemorial antiquity, derived from the oldeſt Theologiſts and Legiſlators, not only in traditions and reports, but in myſteries and ſacrifices, both Greek and Barbarian.* Fire was the efficient principle of both, and, according to ſome of the Ægyptians, that ætherial Fire which concentred in the Sun. This opinion PLUTARCH controverts, ſaying that TYPHON, the evil or deſtroying power, was a terreſtrial or material Fire, eſſentially different from the ætherial. But PLUTARCH here argues from his own prejudices, rather than from the evidence of the caſe; for he believed in an original evil Principle coeternal with the good, and acting in perpetual oppoſition to it; an error into which men have been led by forming falſe notions of good and evil, and conſidering them as ſelf-exiſting inherent properties, inſtead of accidental modifications, variable with every circumſtance with which cauſes and events are connected. This error, though adopted by individuals, never formed a part either of the Theology or Mythology of GREECE. HOMER, in the beautiful allegory of the two Caſks, makes JUPITER, the Supreme God, the diſtributor

‡ *De Iſ. & Oſ.* Ed. Reiſkii.

diſtributor of both good and evil.* The name of JUPITER, Ζευς, was originally one of the titles or epithets of the Sun, ſignifying, according to its etymology, *aweful* or *terrible*†; in which ſenſe it is uſed in the Orphic Litanies.‡ PAN, the Univerſal Subſtance, is called the HORNED JUPITER (Ζευς ὁ κεραστης); and in an Orphic fragment preſerved by MACROBIUS § the names of JUPITER and BACCHUS appear to be only titles of the all-creating power of the Sun.

> Αγλαε Ζευ, Διονυσε, πατερ ποντου, πατερ αιης,
> Ἡλιε παγγενετορ.

In another fragment preſerved by the ſame Author,‖ the name of PLUTO, Αιδης, is uſed as a title of the ſame Deity; who appears therefore to have preſided over the dead as well as over the living, and to have been the Lord of deſtruction as well as creation and preſervation. We accordingly find that in one of the Orphic Litanies now extant he is expreſſly called the Giver of Life, and the Deſtroyer.¶

The

* *Il.* ω. v. 527.

† DAMM. *Lex. Etymol.*

‡ Hymn. X. v. 13.

§ *Sat.* Lib. I. c. 23.

‖ *Sat.* Lib. I. c. 8.

¶ Hymn. lxxii. *Ed. Geſn.*

The Egyptians reprefented TYPHON, the deftroying Power, under the figure of the Hippopotamus or River-Horfe, the moft fierce and deftructive animal they knew;* and the Chorus in the *Bacchæ* of EURIPIDES invoke their infpirer BACCHUS to appear under the form of a Bull, a many-headed Serpent, or flaming Lion;† which fhews that the moft bloody and deftructive, as well as the moft ufeful of animals, was employed by the Greeks to reprefent fome perfonified attribute of the God. M. D'HANCARVILLE has alfo obferved, that the Lion is frequently employed by the ancient Artifts as a fymbol of the Sun;‡ and I am inclined to believe, that it was to exprefs this deftroying Power, no lefs requifite to preferve the harmony of the Univerfe than the generating. In moft of the monuments of ancient art, where the Lion is reprefented, he appears with expreffions of rage and violence, and often in the act of killing and devouring fome other animal. On an ancient Sarcophagus found in SICILY he is reprefented devouring a Horfe,§ and on

* PLUTARCH. *de If. & Of.* † V. 1015.

‡ *Recherches fur les Arts.* See alfo MACROB. *Sat.* I. c. 21.

§ HOUEL, *Voyage de la Sicile.* Plate xxxvi.

on the Medals of VELIA in ITALY, devouring a Deer.* the former, as ſacred to NEPTUNE, repreſented the Sea; and the latter, as ſacred to DIANA, the produce of the Earth; for DIANA was the fertility of the Earth perſonified, and therefore is ſaid to have received her Nymphs or productive Miniſters from the Ocean, the ſource of fecundity.† The Lion therefore, in the former inſtance, appears as a ſymbol of the Sun exhaling the waters; and in the latter, as withering and putrifying the produce of the Earth. On the Frieze of the Temple of APOLLO DIDYMÆUS, near MILETUS, are Monſters compoſed of the mixt forms of the Goat and Lion, reſting their fore feet upon the Lyre of the God, which ſtands between them.§ The Goat, as I have already ſhewn, repreſented the creative Attribute, and the Lyre, Harmony and Order; therefore, if we admit that the Lion repreſented the deſtroying Attribute, this compoſition will ſignify, in the ſymbolical language of ſculpture, the har-

* Plate XI. Fig. 2. engraved from one belonging to me.

† CALLIMACH. *Hymn. ad Dian.* V. 13. *Genitor Nympharum Oceanus.* CATULLUS *in Gell.* V. 84.

§ *Ionian Antiquities,* Vol. I. c. 3. Plate IX.

mony and order of the Univerſe preſerved by the regular and periodical operations of the creative and deſtructive Powers. This is a notion to which men would be naturally led by obſerving the common order and progreſſion of things. The ſame heat of the Sun, which ſcorched and withered the graſs in ſummer, ripened the fruits in autumn, and cloathed the Earth with verdure in the ſpring. In one ſeaſon it dried up the waters from the Earth, and in another returned them in rain. It cauſed fermentation and putrefaction, which deſtroy one generation of plants and animals, and produce another in conſtant and regular ſucceſſion. This contention between the powers of Creation and Deſtruction is repreſented on an ancient Medal of ACANTHUS, in the Muſeum of the late Dr. HUNTER, by a combat between the Bull and Lion.* The Bull alone is repreſented on other medals in exactly the ſame attitude and geſture as when fighting with the Lion;† whence I conclude that the Lion is there underſtood. On the medals of CELENDERIS the Goat

* Plate IX. Fig. 1. & *Nummi vet. Pop. & Urb.* Table I. Fig. 16.

† Plate IX. Fig. 9. from one of ASPENDUS in the ſame Collection. See *Nummi Vet. Pop. & Urb.* Tab. VIII. Fig. 20.

Goat appears instead of the Bull in exactly the same attitude of struggle and contention, but without the Lion;* and in a curious one of very ancient but excellent workmanship, belonging to me, the Ivy of Bacchus is placed over the back of the Goat, to denote the power which he represents.†

The mutual operation, which was the result of this contention, was signified, in the Mythological tales of the Poets, by the Loves of Mars and Venus, the one the active power of Destruction, and the other the passive power of Generation. From their union is said to have sprung the Goddess *Harmony*, who was the physical order of the Universe personified. The fable of Ceres and Proserpine is the same allegory inverted; Ceres being the prolific power of the Earth personified, and hence called by the Greeks *Mother Earth*, (Γη or Δη-μητηρ.) The Latin name Ceres also signifying *Earth*, the Roman C being the same originally both in figure and power as the Greek Γ,‡ which Homer often uses as a mere

* *Nummi Vet. Pop. & Urb.* Tab. XVI. Fig. 13.

† Plate IX. Fig. 10.

‡ See S. C. Marcian. and the Medals of Gela and Agrigentum.

guttural aſpirate, and adds it arbitrarily to his words to make them more ſolemn and ſonorous.* The guttural aſpirates and hiſſing terminations more particularly belonged to the Æolic dialect, from which the Latin was derived ; wherefore we need not wonder, that the ſame word, which by the Dorians and Ionians was written Ερα and Ερε, ſhould by the Æolians be written Γερες or CERES, the Greeks always accommodating their orthography to their pronunciation. In an ancient Bronze at STRAWBERRY-HILL this Goddeſs is repreſented ſitting, with a Cup in one hand, and various ſorts of Fruits in the other ; and the Bull, the emblem of the power of the Creator, in her lap.† This compoſition ſhews the fructification of the Earth by the deſcent of the creative Spirit in the ſame manner as deſcribed by VIRGIL.

> Vere tument terræ, & genitalia ſemina poſcunt ;
> Tum Pater omnipotens fœcundis imbribus æther
> Conjugis in gremium lætæ deſcendit, & omnes
> Magnus alit, magno commixtus corpore, fœtus.‡

Æther and Water are here introduced by the Poet as the two prolific elements, which fertilize the Earth,

---

* As in the word εριδουπος, uſually written by him εριγδουπος.

† See Plate VIII. Fig. 1.

‡ *Georgic.* Lib. II. V. 324.

Earth, according to the ancient Syſtem of the Orphic Philoſophy, upon which the Myſtic Theology was founded. PROSERPINE, or Περσιφονεια, the Daughter of CERES, was, as her Greek name indicates, the Goddeſs of Deſtruction, in which character ſhe is invoked by ALTHÆA in the ninth Iliad: but nevertheleſs we often find her on the Greek medals crowned with Ears of Corn, as being the Goddeſs of Fertility as well as Deſtruction.* She is, in fact, a perſonification of the Heat or Fire that pervades the Earth, which is at once the cauſe and effect of fertility and deſtruction, for it is at once the cauſe and effect of fermentation, from which both proceed. The LIBITINA, or Goddeſs of Death, of the Romans, was the ſame as the PERSIPHONEIA of the Greeks; and yet, as PLUTARCH obſerves, the moſt learned of that people allowed her to be the ſame as VENUS, the Goddeſs of Generation.†

In the Gallery at FLORENCE is a coloſſal image of the Organ of Generation, mounted on the back parts of

* Plate IV. Fig. 5. from a Medal of AGATHOCLES, belonging to me. The ſame head is upon many others, of SYRACUSE, METAPONTUM, &c.

† In NUMA.

of a Lion, and hung round with various animals. By this is reprefented the co-operation of the creating and deftroying Powers, which are both blended and united in one figure, becaufe both are derived from one caufe. The animals hung round fhew likewife, that both act to the fame purpofe, that of replenifhing the Earth, and peopling it with ftill rifing generations of fenfitive beings. The Chimæra of HOMER, of which the Commentators have given fo many whimfical interpretations, was a fymbol of the fame kind, which the Poet, probably, having feen in ASIA, and not knowing its meaning, (which was only revealed to the Initiated) fuppofed to be a monfter, that had once infefted the country. He defcribes it as compofed of the forms of the *Goat*, the *Lion*, and the *Serpent*; and breathing *Fire* from its mouth.* Thefe are the fymbols of the *Creator*, the *Deftroyer*, and the *Preferver*, united and animated by *Fire*, the divine effence of all *Three*.† On a Gem, publifhed in the Memoirs of the Academy of CORTONA,‡ this

---

* *Il* ζ. V. 223.

† For the natural properties attributed by the Ancients to Fire, fee PLUTARCH. *in Camillo*, PLIN. *Hift. Nat.* Lib. xxxvi. c. 68.

‡ Vol. IV. p. 32. See alfo Plate V. Fig. 4. copied from it.

this union of the deſtroying and preſerving Attributes is repreſented by the united forms of the Lion and Serpent crowned with rays, the emblems of the cauſe from which both proceed. This compoſition forms the Chnoubis of the Egyptians.

Bacchus is frequently repreſented by the ancient Artiſts, accompanied by Tigers, which appear, in ſome inſtances, devouring Cluſters of Grapes, the fruit peculiarly conſecrated to the God, and in others drinking the Liquor preſſed from them. The Author of the *Recherches ſur les Arts* has in this inſtance followed the common accounts of the Mythologiſts, and aſſerted that Tigers are really fond of grapes ;* which is ſo far from being true, that they are incapable of feeding upon them, or upon any fruit whatever, being both externally and internally formed to feed upon fleſh only, and to procure their food by deſtroying other animals. Hence I am perſuaded, that in the ancient ſymbols, Tigers, as well as Lions, repreſent the deſtroying power of the God. Sometimes his Chariot appears drawn by them ; and then they repreſent the

* Liv. I. c. 3.

the powers of Deſtruction preceding the powers of Generation, and extending their operation, as putrefaction proceeds, and increaſes vegetation. On a Medal of MARONEA, publiſhed by GESNER,* a Goat is coupled with the Tiger in drawing his Chariot; by which compoſition the Artiſt has ſhewn the *general active* power of the Deity, conducted by his two great attributes of Creation and Deſtruction. On the Choragic monument of LYSICRATES at ATHENS, BACCHUS is repreſented feeding a Tiger; which ſhews the active power of Generation, feeding and cheriſhing the active power of Deſtruction.† On a beautiful Cameo in the collection of the Duke of MARLBOROUGH, the Tiger is ſucking the breaſt of a Nymph; which repreſents the ſame power of Deſtruction, nouriſhed by the paſſive power of Generation.‡ In the Muſeum of CHARLES TOWNLEY, Eſq; is a groupe, in marble, of three figures;§ the middle one of which grows out of a Vine,

* Tab. XLIII. Fig. 26.

† STUART's *Athens*, Vol. I. c. 4. Plate X.

‡ See Plate XVIII. engraved merely to ſhew the compoſition, it not being permitted to make an exact drawing of it.

§ See Plate XIII.

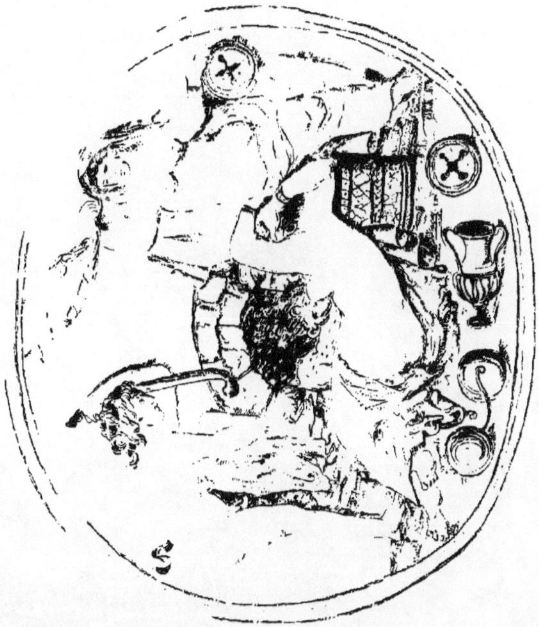

a Vine, in a human form, with leaves and cluſters of grapes ſpringing out of its body. On one ſide is the BACCHUS διφυης, or Creator of both ſexes, known by the effeminate mold of his limbs and countenance; and on the other, a Tiger, leaping up, and devouring the grapes which ſpring from the body of the perſonified Vine, the hands of which are employed in receiving another cluſter from the BACCHUS. This compoſition repreſents the Vine between the creating and deſtroying attributes of God; the one giving it fruit, and the other devouring it when given. The Tiger has a garland of Ivy round his neck, to ſhew that the deſtroyer was co-eſſential with the Creator, of whom Ivy, as well as all other Ever-greens, was an emblem repreſenting his perpetual youth and viridity.*

The mutual and alternate operation of the two great attributes of Creation and Deſtruction, was not confined by the ancients to plants and animals, and ſuch tranſitory productions, but extended to the universe itſelf. Fire being the eſſential cauſe of both, they believed that the conflagration and renovation

* STRABO, Lib. XV. p. 712.

of the world were periodical and regular, proceeding from each other by the laws of its own conſtitution, implanted in it by the Creator, who was alſo the Deſtroyer and Renovator;* for, as PLATO ſays, all things ariſe from one, and into one are all things reſolved.† It muſt be obſerved, that, when the ancients ſpeak of creation and deſtruction, they mean only formation and diſſolution; it being univerſally allowed, through all ſyſtems of religion, or ſects of philoſophy, that *nothing could come from nothing, and that no power whatever could annihilate that which really exiſted.* The bold and magnificent idea of a creation from nothing was reſerved for the more vigorous faith, and more enlightened minds, of the moderns,‡ who need ſeek no authority to confirm their belief; for, as that which is ſelf-evident admits of no

* BRUCKER, *Hiſt. Crit. Philoſ.* Vol. I. part ii. lib. 1. PLUTARCH. *de Placit. Philoſ.* Lib. II. c. 18. LUCRETIUS, Lib. V. ver. 92. CIC. *de Nat. Deor.* Lib. II.

† Εξ ἑνος τα παντα γινεσθαι, και εις τ' αυτον αναλυεσθαι in PHÆD. The ſame Dogma is ſtill more plainly inculcated of the ancient Indian Author before cited, ſee *Bagvat Geeta,* Lect. ix.

‡ The word in *Geneſis* upon which it is founded, conveyed no ſuch ſenſe to the ancients; for the Seventy tranſlated it εποιησε, which ſignifies *formed*, or *faſhioned*.

no proof, so that which is in itself impossible admits of no refutation.

The fable of the Serpent PYTHO being destroyed by APOLLO, probably arose from an emblematical composition, in which that God was represented as the destroyer of Life, of which the Serpent was a symbol. PLINY mentions a statue of him by PRAXITELES, which was much celebrated in his time, called Σαυροκτον *(the Lizard-killer.*)* The Lizard, being supposed to live upon the dews and moisture of the earth, is employed as the symbol of Humidity in general; so that the God destroying it, signifies the same as the Lion devouring the Horse. The title APOLLO, I am inclined to believe, meant originally the Destroyer, as well as the Deliverer; for, as the ancients supposed destruction to be merely dissolution, the power which delivered the particles of matter from the bonds of attraction, and broke the δεσμον περιεργιδη ερωτος, was in fact the Destroyer.† It

 is,

* *Hist. Nat.* Lib. XXXIV. c. 8. Many copies of it are still extant. WINKELMAN has published one from a bronze of Cardinal ALBANI's. *Monum. Antichi inediti*, Pl. XL.

† The verb λυω, from which APOLLO is derived, signifies in HOMER both to *free*, and to dissolve or destroy. Il. α, ver. 20. Il. ι, ver. 25. MACROBIUS derives the title from απολλυμι, to *destroy*; but this word is derived from λυω. Sat. Lib. I. c. 17.

is, probably, for this reason, that sudden death, plagues, and epidemic diseases, are said by the Poets to be sent by this God ; who is, at the same time, described as the Author of Medicine, and all the arts employed to preserve life. These attributes are not joined merely because the destroyer and preserver were essentially the same ; but because disease necessarily precedes cure, and is the cause of its being invented. The God of Health is said to be his son, because the health and vigour of one being are supported by the decay and dissolution of others which are appropriated to its nourishment. The Bow and Arrows are given to him as symbols of his characteristic attributes, as they are to DIANA, who was the female personification of the destructive, as well as the productive and preserving powers. DIANA is hence called the triple HECATE, and represented by three female bodies joined together. Her attributes were however worshipped separately ; and some nations revered her under one character, and others under another. DIANA of EPHESUS was the productive and nutritive Power, as the many Breasts and other symbols on her statues imply ;* whilst Βριμω, the

* HIERON. *Comment. in* PAUL. *Epist. ad Ephes.*

the *Tauric* or *Scythic* DIANA, appears to have been the deſtructive, and therefore was appeaſed with human ſacrifices, and other bloody rites.* She is repreſented ſometimes ſtanding on the back of a Bull,† and ſometimes in a Chariot drawn by Bulls;‡ whence ſhe is called by the Poets Ταυροπολα§ and Βοων ελατειρα.‖ Both compoſitions ſhew the paſſive power of Nature, whether creative or deſtructive, ſuſtained and guided by the general active power of the Creator, of which the Sun was the centre, and the Bull the ſymbol.

It was obſerved by the ancients, that the deſtructive power of the Sun was exerted moſt by day, and the creative by night: for it was in the former ſeaſon that he dried up the waters, withered the herbs, and produced diſeaſe and putrefaction; and in the latter, that he returned the exhalations in dews, tempered with

---

* PAUSAN. Lib. III. c. 16.

† See a medal of AUGUSTUS, publiſhed by SPANHEIM. *Not. in* CALLIM. *Hymn. ad* DIAN. Ver. 113.

‡ Plate VI. from a bronze in the Muſeum of C. TOWNLEY, Eſq.

§ SOPHOCLIS *Ajax*, Ver. 172.

‖ *Nonni* DIONYS. Lib. I. the title Ταυροπολος was ſometimes given to APOLLO, EUSTATH. *Schol. in* DIONYS. περιηγητ. Ver. 609.

with the genial heat which he had transfused into the atmosphere, to restore and replenish the waste of the day. Hence, when they personified the attributes, they revered the one as the *diurnal*, and the other as the *nocturnal* Sun, and in their mystic worship, as MACROBIUS says,* called the former APOLLO, and the latter DIONYSIUS or BACCHUS. The mythological personages of CASTOR and POLLUX, who lived and died alternately, were allegories of the same dogma; hence the two Asterises, by which they are distinguished on the medals of LOCRI, ARGOS, and other Cities.

The Pæans, or war-songs, which the Greeks chanted at the onset of their battles,† were originally sung to APOLLO,‡ who was called PÆON; and MACROBIUS tells us,§ that in SPAIN, the Sun was worshipped as MARS, the God of War and Destruction, whose statue they adorned with Rays, like that of the Greek APOLLO. On a Celtiberian or Runic medal found in SPAIN, of barbarous workmanship, is a head

* SAT. Lib. I. c. 18.
† THUCYD. Lib. VII.
‡ HOMER. *Il.* α. V. 472.
§ SAT. Lib. I. c. 19.

Plate XIV.

Fig. 3

Fig. 1

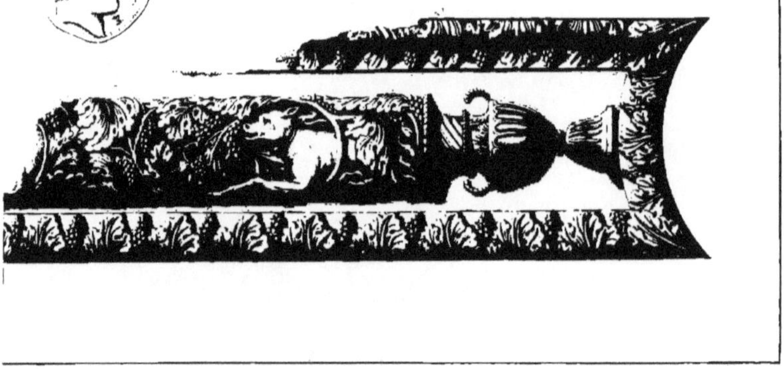

Fig. 2

a head ſurrounded by Obeliſcs or Rays, which I take to be of this Deity.* The hairs appear erect, to imitate flames, as they do on many of the Greek medals; and on the reverſe is a bearded head, with a ſort of pyramidal cap on, exactly reſembling that by which the Romans conferred freedom on their ſlaves, and which was therefore called the Cap of Liberty.† On other Celtiberian medals is a figure on horſeback, carrying a ſpear in his hand, and having the ſame ſort of cap on his head, with the word HELMAN written under him,‡ in characters which are ſomething between the old Runic, and Pelaſgian; but ſo near to the latter, that they are eaſily underſtood.§ This figure ſeems to be of the ſame perſon

as

---

* Plate IX. Fig. 12. engraved from one belonging to me. I have ſince been confirmed in this conjecture by obſerving the characters of MARS and APOLLO mixt on Greek coins. On a Mamertine one belonging to me is a head with the youthful features and Laurel Crown of APOLLO; but the hair is ſhort, and the inſcription on the exergue denotes it to be MARS. See Plate XIV. Fig. 3.

† It may be ſeen with the Dagger on the medals of BRUTUS.

‡ See Plate IX. Fig. 6. from one belonging to me.

§ The firſt is a mixture of the Runic *Hagle* and Greek Π. The ſecond is the Runic *Laugur*, which is alſo the old Greek Λ, as it appears on the Vaſe of the Calydonian Boar in the BRITISH MUSEUM. The other three differ little from the common Greek.

as is reprefented by the head with the cap on the preceding Medal, who can be no other than the Angel or Minifter of the Deity of Death, as the name implies; for HELA, or HEL, was, among the Northern nations, the Goddefs of Death,* in the fame manner as PERSIPHONEIA or BRIMO was among the Greeks. The fame figure appears on many ancient Britifh medals, and alfo on thofe of feveral Greek Cities, particularly thofe of GELA, which have the Taurine BACCHUS or Creator on the reverfe.† The head which I have fuppofed to be the Celtiberian MARS, or deftructive power of the diurnal Sun, is beardlefs like the APOLLO of the Greeks, and, as far as can be difcovered in fuch barbarous fculpture, has the fame Androgynous features‡ We may therefore reafonably fuppofe, that, like the Greeks, the Celtiberians perfonified the deftructive attribute under the different genders, accordingly as they applied it to the Sun, or fubordinate elements; and then united them,

* EDDA, Fab. xvi. D'HANCARVILLE, *Recherches fur les Arts*, Liv. II. c. 1.

† See Plate IX. Fig. 8. from one belonging to me.

‡ See Plate IX. Fig. 2.

them, to ſignify that both were eſſentially the ſame. The HELMAN therefore, who was the ſame as the Μοιραγητης or Διακτωρ of the Greeks, may with equal propriety be called the Miniſter of *both*, or *either*. The Spear in his hand is not to be conſidered merely as the implement of Deſtruction, but as the ſymbol of Power and Command, which it was in GREECE and ITALY, as well as all over the North. Hence ευθυνειν δορι, was *to govern*,* and *venire ſub haſtâ*,—*to be ſold as a ſlave*. The ancient Celtes and Scythians paid divine honours to the Sword, the Battle-axe, and the Spear; the firſt of which was the ſymbol by which they repreſented the Supreme God: hence to ſwear by the Edge of the Sword was the moſt ſacred and inviolable of oaths.† EURIPIDES alludes to this ancient religion when he calls a ſword ὁρκιον ξιφος; and ÆSCHYLUS ſhewed clearly, that it once prevailed in GREECE, when he makes the Heroes of the THEBAID ſwear by the Point of the Spear (ομνυσι δ'αιχμην.)‡ HOMER ſometimes uſes the word αρης to ſignify the God of War,

* EURIP. *Hecuba*.

† MALLET, *Introd. à l'Hiſt. de Danemarc*, c. 9.

‡ Ἑπτα επι Θηβας. V. 535.

and ſometimes a Weapon: and we have ſufficient proof of this word's being of Celtic origin in its affinity with our Northern word *War*; for, if we write it in the ancient manner, with the Pelaſgian *Vau*, or Æolian *Digamma*, Ϝαρης *(Wares)*, it ſcarcely differs at all.

Behind the bearded Head, on the firſt-mentioned Celtiberian medal, is an inſtrument like a pair of Fire-tongs, or Blackſmith's Pincers;* from which it ſeems, that the perſonage here repreſented is the ſame as the Ἡφαιστος or VULCAN of the Greek and Roman Mythology. The ſame ideas are expreſſed ſomewhat more plainly on the medals of ÆSERNIA in ITALY, which are executed with all the refinement and elegance of Grecian art.† On one ſide is APOLLO, the diurnal Sun, mounting in his Chariot; and on the other, a beardleſs Head, with the ſame Cap on, and the ſame inſtrument behind it; but with the youthſul features, and elegant character of countenance, uſually attributed to MERCURY, who, as well as VULCAN, was the God of Art and Mechaniſm;

* Plate IX. Fig. 12.

† See Plate IX. Fig. 15. from one belonging to me.

Mechanism; and whose peculiar office it also was, to conduct the souls of the deceased to their eternal mansions; from whence came the epithet Διακτωρ, applied to him by HOMER. He was therefore, in this respect, the same as the HELMAN of the Celtes and Scythians, who was supposed to conduct the souls of all who died a violent death (which alone was accounted truly happy) to the Palace of VALHALA.* It seems that the attributes of the Deity, which the Greeks represented by the mythological personages of VULCAN and MERCURY, were united in the Celtic mythology. CÆSAR tells us, that the Germans worshipped VULCAN, or Fire, with the Sun and Moon; and I shall soon have occasion to shew, that the Greeks held Fire to be the real conductor of the dead, and emancipator of the soul. The Æsernians, bordering upon the Samnites, a Celtic nation, might naturally be supposed to have adopted the notions of their neighbours, or, what is more probable, preserved the religion of their ancestors more pure than the Hellenic Greeks. Hence they represented VULCAN, who, from the inscription on the exergue of their coins, appears to have been

* MALLET, *Hist. de Danemarc. Introd.* c. 9.

their tutelar God, with the characteriſtic features of MERCURY, who was only a different perſonification of the ſame Deity.

At LYCOPOLIS in EGYPT, the deſtroying power of the Sun was repreſented by a Wolf; which, as MACROBIUS ſays, was worſhipped there as APOLLO.* The Wolf appears devouring Grapes in the ornaments of the temple of BACCHUS περικιονιος at PUZZUOLI;† and on the medals of CARTHA he is ſurrounded with Rays; which plainly proves that he is there meant as a ſymbol of the Sun.‡ He is alſo repreſented on moſt of the coins of ARGOS,§ where I have already ſhewn that the diurnal Sun APOLLO, the light-extending God, was peculiarly worſhipped. We may therefore conclude, that this animal is meant for one of the myſtic ſymbols of the primitive worſhip; and not, as ſome Antiquarians have ſuppoſed, to commemorate the mythological tales of DANAUS or LYCAON, which were probably invented, like many others of the

* Sat. Lib. I. c. 17. † Plate XIV. Fig. 1.

‡ Plate IX. Fig. 18, from one belonging to me.

§ Plate IX. Fig. 4. from one belonging to me.

the ſame kind, to ſatisfy the inquiſitive ignorance of the vulgar, from whom the meaning of the myſtic ſymbols, the uſual devices on the medals, was ſtrictly concealed. In the Celtic Mythology, the ſame ſymbol was employed, apparently in the ſame ſenſe; Lok, the great deſtroying Power of the univerſe, being repreſented under the form of a Wolf.*

The Apollo Didymæus, or *double Apollo*, was probably the two perſonifications, that of the *deſtroying*, and that of the creating power, united; whence we may perceive the reaſon why the ornaments before deſcribed ſhould be upon his temple.† On the medals of Antigonus, King of Asia, is a figure, with his hair hanging in artificial ringlets over his ſhoulders, like that of a woman; and the whole compoſition, both of his limbs and countenance, remarkable for extreme delicacy, and feminine elegance.‡ He is ſitting on the prow of a ſhip, as God of the Waters; and we ſhould, without heſitation, pronounce

* Mallet, *Introd. à l'Hiſt. de Danemarc.*

† See *Ionian Antiq.* Vol. I. c. 3. Pl. IX.

‡ See Plate IX. Fig. 16. from one belonging to me. Similar figures are on the coins of moſt of the Seleucidæ.

pronounce him to be the BACCHUS διφυης, were it not for the Bow that he carries in his hand, which evidently ſhews him to be APOLLO. This I take to be the figure under which the refinement of art (and more was never ſhewn than in this Medal) repreſented the APOLLO DYDYMÆUS, or union of the creative and deſtructive powers of both ſexes in one body.

As Fire was the primary eſſence of the active or male powers of Creation and Generation, ſo was Water of the paſſive or female. APPIAN ſays, that the Goddeſs worſhipped at HIERAPOLIS in SYRIA was *called by ſome* VENUS, *by others* JUNO, *and by others held to be the cauſe which produced the beginning and ſeeds of things from humidity.** PLUTARCH deſcribes her nearly in the ſame words;† and the Author of the Treatiſe attributed to LUCIAN‡ ſays, *ſhe was Nature, the Parent of things, or the Creatreſs.* She was therefore the ſame as ISIS, who was the prolific material, upon which both the creative and deſtructive Attributes operated.§ As Water was her terreſtrial eſſence, ſo was the Moon her celeſtial image, whoſe attractive power,

* *De Bello Parthico.*

† *In Craſſo.*

‡ *De Dea Syria.*

§ PLUTARCH. *de Iſ. & Oſ.*

power, heaving the waters of the Ocean, naturally led men to associate them. The Moon was also supposed to return the dews which the Sun exhaled from the Earth; and hence her warmth was reckoned to be moistening, as that of the Sun was drying.* The Egyptians called her the Mother of the World, because she sowed and scattered into the air the prolific principles, with which she had been impregnated by the Sun.† These principles, as well as the light by which she was illumined, being supposed to emanate from the great fountain of all life and motion, partook of the nature of the being from which they were derived. Hence the Egyptians attributed to the Moon, as well as to the Sun, the active and passive powers of Generation,‡ which were both, to use the language of the Scholastics, *essentially* the same, though *formally* different. This union is represented on a medal of DEMETRIUS the second King of SYRIA,§ where the Goddess of HIERAPOLIS appears with

* *Calor Solis arefacit, Lunaris humectat.* MACROB. *Sat.* VII. c. 10.

† PLUTARCH. *de Is. & Os.*

‡ *Ibid.*

§ Plate IX. Fig. 14. from HAYM *Tes. Brit.* p. 70.

with the Male Organs of Generation ſticking out of her robe, and holding the Thyrſus of BACCHUS, the emblem of Fire, in one hand, and the terreſtrial Globe, repreſenting the ſubordinate elements, in the other. Her head is crowned with various plants, and on each ſide is an Aſteriſc repreſenting (probably) the diurnal and nocturnal Sun, in the ſame manner as when placed over the caps of CASTOR and POLLUX.* This is not the form under which ſhe was repreſented in the Temple at HIERAPOLIS, when the Author of the account attributed to LUCIAN viſited it; which is not to be wondered at, for the figures of this univerſal Goddeſs, being merely emblematical, were compoſed according to the attributes which the Artiſts meant particularly to expreſs. She is probably repreſented here in the form under which ſhe was worſhipped in the neighbourhood of CYZICUS, where ſhe was called Αρτεμις Πριαπινη, the *Priapic Diana*.† In the Temple at HIERAPOLIS the active powers imparted to her by the Creator were repreſented by immenſe images of the Male Organs of Generation placed on each ſide of the door. The meaſures of theſe muſt neceſſarily

* See Plate IX. Fig. 4. † PLUTARCH. *in Lucullo.*

neceſſarily be corrupt in the preſent text of LUCIAN; but that they were of an enormous ſize, we may conclude from what is related of a Man's going to the top of one of them every year, and reſiding there ſeven days, in order to have a more intimate communication with the Deity, while praying for the proſperity of SYRIA.* ATHENÆUS relates, that PTOLEMY PHILADELPHUS had one of 120 cubits long, carried in proceſſion at ALEXANDRIA,† of which the Poet might juſtly have ſaid

——— horrendum protendit Mentula contum
Quanta queat vaſtos Thetidis ſpumantis hiatus;
Quanta queat priſcamque Rheam, magnamque Parentem
Naturam, ſolidis naturam implere medullis,
Si foret immenſos, quot ad aſtra volantia currunt,
Conceptura globos, & tela triſulca Tonantis,
Et vaga concuſſum motura tonitrua mundum.

This was the real meaning of the enormous figures at HIERAPOLIS:—they were the Generative Organs of the Creator perſonified, with which he was ſuppoſed to have impregnated the Heavens, the Earth, and the Waters. Within the Temple were many ſmall ſtatues of Men with theſe Organs diſproportionably large.

* LUCIAN. *de Dea Syria.* † *Deipnoſ.* Lib.

large. Thefe were the Angels or attendants of the Goddefs, who acted as her Minifters of Creation in peopling and fructifying the Earth. The ftatue of the Goddefs herfelf was in the Sanctuary of the Temple; and near it was the ftatue of the Creator, whom the Author calls JUPITER, as he does the Goddefs, JUNO; by which he only means that they were the Supreme Deities of the country where worfhipped. She was borne by Lions, and He by Bulls, to fhew that Nature, the paffive productive Power of matter, was fuftained by anterior deftruction, whilft the Ætherial Spirit, or active productive Power, was fuftained by his own ftrength only, of which the Bulls were fymbols.* Between both was a third Figure, with a Dove on his head, which fome thought to be BACCHUS.† This was the Holy Spirit, the firft-begotten Love, or plaftic Nature, (of which the Dove was the image, when it really deigned to defcend upon Man‡) proceeding from, and

* The *active* and *paffive* Powers of Creation are called *Male* and *Female* by the Ammonian Platonics. See PROCLUS *in Theol. Platon.* Lib. I. c. 28.

† LUCIAN. *de Dea Syriâ.*

‡ MATTH. c. iii. ver. 17.

and consubstantial with *Both*; for all *Three* were but personifications of *One*. The Dove, or some Fowl like it, appears on the medals of GORTYNA in CRETE, acting the same part with DICTYNNA, the Cretan DIANA, as the Swan is usually represented acting with LEDA.* This composition has nearly the same signification as that before described of the Bull in the lap of CERES, DIANA being equally a personification of the productive power of the Earth. It may seem extraordinary, that after this adventure with the Dove, she should still remain a Virgin; but mysteries of this kind are to be found in all religions. JUNO is said to have renewed her virginity every year by bathing in a certain Fountain;† a miracle which I believe even modern legends cannot parallel.

In the Vision of EZEKIEL, God is described as descending upon the combined forms of the Eagle, the Bull, and the Lion,* the emblems of the Æthe-

---

* See Plate X. Fig. 2. Καλουσι δε την Αρτεμιν Θρακες Βενδειαν, Κρητες δε Δικτυνναν. PALÆPH. *de Incred.* Tab. XXXI. See also DIODOR. SIC. Lib. V. & EURIPID. *Hippol.* V. 145.

† PAUSAN. Lib. II. c. 38.

‡ EZEK. c. i. v. 10. with LOWTH's *Comm.*

rial Spirit, the Creative and Deſtructive Powers, which were all united in the true God, though hypoſtatically divided in the Syrian Trinity. Man was compounded with them, as repreſenting the real image of God, according to the Jewiſh Theology. The Cherubim on the Ark of the Covenant, between which God dwelt,* were alſo compounded of the ſame forms,† ſo that the idea of them muſt have been preſent to the Prophet's mind, previous to the Apparition which furniſhed him with the deſcription. Even thoſe on the Ark of the Covenant, though made at the expreſs command of God, do not appear to have been original; for a figure exactly anſwering to the deſcription of them appears among thoſe curious ruins exiſting at CHILMINAR, in PERSIA, which have been ſuppoſed to be thoſe of the Palace of PERSEPOLIS, burnt by ALEXANDER; but for what reaſon, it is not eaſy to conjecture. They do not, certainly, anſwer to any ancient deſcription extant, of that celebrated palace; but, as far as we can judge of them in their preſent ſtate, appear evidently to

* *Exod.* ch. xxv. ver. 22.

† SPENCER *de Leg. Ritual. Vet. Hebræor.* Lib. III. Diſſert. 5.

to have been a Temple.* But the Perſians, as before obſerved, had no incloſed temples or ſtatues, which they held in ſuch abhorrence, that they tried every means poſſible to deſtroy thoſe of the Egyptians; thinking it unworthy of the majeſty of the Deity to have his all-pervading preſence limited to the boundary of an edifice, or likened to an image of ſtone or metal. Yet, among the ruins at CHILMINAR, we not only find many ſtatues, which are evidently of ideal beings,† but alſo that remarkable emblem of the Deity, which diſtinguiſhes almoſt all the Egyptian temples now extant.‡ The portals are alſo of the ſame form as thoſe at THEBES and PHILÆ; and, except the hieroglyphics which diſtinguiſh the latter, are finiſhed and ornamented nearly in the ſame manner. Unleſs, therefore, we ſuppoſe the Perſians to have been ſo inconſiſtent as to erect temples in direct contradiction to the firſt principles of

* See LE BRUYN, *Voyage en Perſe*, Planche cxxiii.

† See LE BRUYN and NIEBUHR.

‡ See Plate XV. Fig. 1. from the Iſiac Table, and Fig 13. from NIEBUHR's Prints of CHILMINAR. See alſo Fig. 2. and 3. from the Iſiac Tables and the Egyptian Portals publiſhed by NORDEN and POCOCKE, on every one of which this ſingular emblem occurs.

of their own religion, and decorate them with ſymbols and images, which they held to be impious and abominable, we cannot ſuppoſe them to be the authors of theſe buildings. Neither can we ſuppoſe the Parthians, or later Perſians, to have been the builders of them; for both the ſtyle of workmanſhip in the figures, and the forms of the letters in the inſcriptions, denote a much higher antiquity, as will appear evidently to any one who will take the trouble of comparing the Drawings publiſhed by Le Bruyn and Niebuhr with the Coins of the Arsacidæ and Sassanidæ. Almoſt all the ſymbolical figures are to be found repeated upon different Phœnician coins; but the letters of the Phœnicians, which are ſaid to have come to them from the Aſſyrians, are much leſs ſimple, and evidently belong to an alphabet much further advanced in improvement. Some of the figures are alſo obſervable upon the Greek coins, particularly the Bull and Lion fighting, and the myſtic Flower, which is the conſtant device of the Rhodians. The ſtyle of workmanſhip is alſo exactly the ſame as that of the very ancient Greek coins of Acanthus, Celendaris, and Lesbos; the lines being very ſtrongly marked, and the hair expreſſed by round knobs. The wings likewiſe of the figure, which

which resembles the Jewish Cherubim, are the same as those upon several Greek sculptures now extant; such as the little images of PRIAPUS attached to the ancient bracelets, the compound figures of the Goat and Lion upon the frieze of the Temple of APOLLO DYDYMÆUS, &c. &c.* They are likewise joined to the human figure on the medals of MELITA and CAMARINA,† as well as upon many ancient sculptures in relief found in PERSIA.‡ The feathers in these wings are turned upwards like those of an Ostrich,§ to which however they have no resemblance in form, but seem rather like those of a Fowl brooding, though more distorted than any I ever observed in Nature. Whether this distortion was meant to express lust or incubation, I cannot determine; but the compositions, to which the wings are added, leave little doubt, that it was meant for the one or the other. I am inclined to believe that it was for the latter, as

---

* See LE BRUYN, Planche CXXIII. *Ionian Antiquities*, Vol. I. c. 3. Plate IX. and the head-piece to Sir *W. H.*'s Letter, Fig. 2.

† See Plate XV. Fig. 11, from one of MELITA, belonging to me.

‡ See LE BRUYN, Planche CXXI.

§ As those on Figures described by EZEKIEL were. See c. i. ver. 11.

as we find on the medals of MELITA, a Figure with four of these wings, who seems by his attitude to be brooding over something.* On his head is the Cap of Liberty, whilst in his right hand he holds the Hook or Attractor, and in his left the Winnow or Separator; so that he probably represents the Ερως or Generative Spirit brooding over matter, and giving liberty to its productive powers by the exertion of his own attributes, Attraction and Separation. On a very ancient Phœnician medal brought from ASIA by Mr. PULLENGER, and published very incorrectly by Mr. SWINTON in the Philosophical Transactions of 1760, is a Disc or Ring surrounded by Wings of different forms, of which some of the feathers are distorted in the same manner.† The same Disc, surrounded by the same kind of Wings, incloses the Asterisc of the Sun over the Bull APIS, or MNEVIS, on the Isiac Table,‡ where it also appears with many of the other Egyptian symbols, particularly over the heads of ISIS and

* See Plate XV. Fig. 11. engraved from one belonging to me.

† See Plate IX. Fig. 6. engraved from the original Medal, now belonging to me.

‡ See Plate XV. Fig. 2. from PIGNORIUS.

and OSIRIS.* It is alſo placed over the entrances of moſt of the Egyptian Temples deſcribed by POCOCKE and NORDEN as well as on that repreſented on the Iſiac Table,† though with ſeveral variations, and without the Aſteriſc. We find it equally without the Aſteriſc, but with little or no variation, on the ruins at CHILMENAR, and other ſuppoſed Perſian antiquities in that neighbourhood:‡ but upon ſome of the Greek medals the Aſteriſc alone is placed over the Bull with the human face,§ who is then the ſame as the APIS or MNEVIS of the Egyptians; that is, the image of the Generative Power of the Sun, which is ſignified by the Aſteriſc on the Greek medals, and by the Kneph, or winged Diſk, on the Oriental monuments. The Greeks however ſometimes employed this latter ſymbol, but contrived, according to their uſual practice, to join it to the human figure, as may be

U ſeen

* See Plate XV. Fig. 3, from PIGNORIUS.

† See Plate XV. Fig. 1, from PIGNORIUS.

‡ See NIEBUHR and LE BRUYN, and Plate XV. Fig. 13, from the former.

§ See Plate IV. Fig. 2, and Plate XV. Fig. 6, from a medal of CALES, belonging to me.

ſeen on a medal of CAMARINA, publiſhed by Prince TORREMMUZZI.* On other medals of this City the ſame idea is expreſſed, without the Diſc or Aſteriſc, by a winged figure, which appears hovering over a Swan, the emblem of the Waters, to ſhew the Generative Power of the Sun fructifying that element, or adding the *active* to the *paſſive* Powers of Production.† On the medals of NAPLES, a winged figure of the ſame kind is repreſented crowning the Taurine BACCHUS with a Wreath of Laurel.‡ This Antiquarians have called a Victory crowning the Minotaur; but the fabulous monſter called the Minotaur was never ſaid to have been victorious, even by the Poets who invented it; and whenever the Sculptors and Painters repreſented it, they joined the head of a Bull to a Human Body, as may be ſeen in the celebrated picture of THESEUS, publiſhed among the antiquities of HERCULANEUM, and on the medals of ATHENS, ſtruck about the time of SEVERUS, when the ſtyle of art was totally changed, and the myſtic theology extinct.

* See Plate XVI. Fig. 2. copied from it.

† See Plate XVI. Fig. 3. from one belonging to me.

‡ See Plate XV. Fig. 7. The coins are common in all collections.

tinct. The winged figure, which has been called a Victory, appears mounting in the Chariot of the Sun, on the medals of Queen PHILISTIS,* and, on some of those of SYRACUSE, flying before it in the place where the Asterisc appears on others of the same city.† I am therefore persuaded, that these are only different modes of representing one idea, and that the winged figure means the same, when placed over the Taurine BACCHUS of the Greeks, as the winged Disc does over the APIS or MNEVIS of the Egyptians. The Ægis, or Snaky Breast-plate, and the MEDUSA's Head, are also, as Dr. STUKELEY justly observed,‡ Greek modes of representing this winged Disc joined with the Serpents, as it frequently is, both in the Egyptian sculptures, and those of CHILMENAR in PERSIA. The expressions of rage and violence, which usually characterise the countenance of the MEDUSA, signify the Destroying attribute joined with the Generative, as both were equally under the direction of MINERVA, or Divine Wisdom. I am in-

 clined

* See Plate XVI. Fig. 4, from one belonging to me.

† See Plate XVI. Fig. 5 and 6, from coins belonging to me

‡ ABURY, p. 93.

clined to believe, that the large Rings, to which the little figures of PRIAPUS are attached,* had alſo the ſame meaning as the Diſc; for, if intended merely to ſuſpend them by, they are of an extravagant magnitude, and would not anſwer their purpoſe ſo well as a common loop.

On the Phœnician coin above mentioned, this ſymbol, the winged Diſc, is placed over a figure ſitting, who holds in his hands an Arrow, whilſt a Bow, ready bent, of the ancient Scythian form, lies by him.† On his head is a large looſe Cap, tied under his chin, which I take to be the Lion's ſkin, worn in the ſame manner as on the heads of HERCULES, upon the medals of ALEXANDER; but the work is ſo ſmall, though executed with extreme nicety and preciſion, and perfectly preſerved, that it is difficult to decide with certainty what it repreſents, in parts of ſuch minuteneſs. The Bow and Arrows, we know, were the ancient arms of HERCULES; and continued ſo, until the Greek Poets thought

* See Plate II. Fig. 1. and Plate III. Fig. 2.

† See Plate IX. Fig. 7. *b*.

‡ HOMER's *Odyſſ.* Λ. ver. 606.

thought proper to give him the Club.* He was particularly worſhipped at TYRE, the metropolis of PHOENICIA;† and his head appears in the uſual form, on many of the coins of that people. We may hence conclude that he is the perſon here repreſented, notwithſtanding the difference in the ſtyle and compoſition of the figure, which may be accounted for by the difference of art. The Greeks, animated by the ſpirit of their ancient poets, and the glowing melody of their language, were grand and poetical in all their compoſitions; whilſt the Phœnicians, who ſpoke a harſh and untuneable dialect, were unacquainted with fine poetry, and conſequently with poetical ideas; for words being the types of ideas, and the ſigns or marks by which men not only communicate them to each other, but arrange and regulate them in their own minds, the genius of a language goes a great way towards forming the character of the people who uſe it. Poverty of expreſſion will produce poverty of conception; for men will never be able to form ſublime ideas, when

* STRABO, Lib. XIV.

† MACROB. *Sat.* Lib. I. c. 20.

when the language in which they *think* (for men always think as well as ſpeak in ſome language) is incapable of expreſſing them. This may be one reaſon why the Phœnicians never rivaled the Greeks in the perfection of art, although they attained a degree of excellence long before them; for HOMER, whenever he has occaſion to ſpeak of any fine piece of art, takes care to inform us that it was the work of Sidonians. He alſo mentions the Phœnician merchants bringing toys and ornaments of dreſs to ſell to the Greeks, and practiſing thoſe frauds which merchants and factors are apt to practiſe upon ignorant people.* It is probable that their progreſs in the fine arts, like that of the Dutch, (who are the Phœnicians of modern hiſtory) never went beyond a ſtrict imitation of nature; which, compared to the more elevated graces of ideal compoſition, is like a news-paper narrative compared with one of HOMER's Battles. A figure of HERCULES, therefore, executed by a Phœnician artiſt, if compared to one by PHIDIAS or LYSIPPUS, would be like a picture of MOSES or DAVID, painted by TENIERS, or GERARD DOW, compared

* HOMER. *Odyſſ.* o. ver. 414.

compared to one of the ſame, painted by RAPHAEL or ANNIBAL CARACCI. This is exactly the difference between the figures on the Medal now under conſideration, and thoſe on the coins of GELO or ALEXANDER. Of all the perſonages of the ancient mythology, HERCULES is perhaps the moſt difficult to explain; for phyſical allegory and fabulous hiſtory are ſo entangled in the accounts we have of him, that it is ſcarcely poſſible to ſeparate them. He appears however, like all the other Gods, to have been originally a perſonified attribute of the Sun. The eleventh of the Orphic Hymns* is addreſſed to him as the Strength and Power of the Sun; and MACROBIUS ſays that he was thought to be the Strength and Virtue of the Gods, by which they deſtroyed the Giants; and that, according to VARRO, the MARS and HERCULES of the Romans were the ſame Deity, and worſhipped with the ſame rites.† According to VARRO then, whoſe authority is perhaps the greateſt that can be cited, HERCULES was the Deſtroying Attribute repreſented in a human form, inſtead of that of a Lion, Tiger, or Hippopotamus. Hence the terrible picture drawn of him by HOMER, which

* *Ed. Geſner.* † *Sat.* Lib. I. c. 20.

which always appeared to me to have been taken from ſome ſymbolical ſtatue, which the Poet not underſtanding, ſuppoſed to be of the Theban Hero, who had aſſumed the title of the Deity, and whoſe fabulous hiſtory he was well acquainted with. The deſcription however applies in every particular to the allegorical perſonage. His attitude, for ever fixed in the act of letting fly his Arrow,* with the figures of Lions and Bears, Battles and Murders, which adorn his Belt, all unite in repreſenting him as the Deſtructive Attribute perſonified. But how happens it then that he is ſo frequently repreſented ſtrangling the Lion, the natural emblem of this power? Is this an hiſtorical fable belonging to the Theban Hero, or a phyſical allegory of the Deſtructive Power deſtroying its own force by its own exertions? Or is the ſingle Attribute perſonified taken for the whole power of the Deity in this, as in other inſtances already mentioned? The Orphic Hymn above cited ſeems to favour this laſt conjecture; for he is there addreſſed both as the Devourer and Generator of all (Παμφαγι παγγενετωρ). However this may be, we may ſafely conclude

* Αιει βαλεοντι ἑοικως. *Odyſſ.* λ. v. 607.

clude that the HERCULES armed with the Bow and Arrow, as he appears on the present medal, is like the APOLLO, the Destroying Power of the diurnal Sun.

On the other side of the Medal* is a figure, somewhat like the JUPITER on the medals of ALEXANDER and ANTIOCHUS, sitting with a beaded Sceptre in his right hand, which he rests upon the head of a Bull, that projects from the side of the Chair. Above, on his right shoulder, is a Bird, probably a Dove, the symbol of the Holy Spirit, descending from the Sun; but, as this part of the medal is less perfect than the rest, the species cannot be clearly discovered. In his left hand he holds a short Staff, from the upper side of which springs an Ear of Corn, and from the lower a Bunch of Grapes, which, being the two most esteemed productions of the Earth, were the natural emblems of general Fertilization. This figure is therefore the Generator, as that on the other side is the Destroyer, whilst the Sun, of whose Attributes both are personifications, is placed between them. The letters on the side of the Generator are

* See Plate IX. Fig. 7. *a*.

quite entire, and, according to the Phœnician alphabet published by Mr. DUTENS, are equivalent to the Roman ones, which compose the words *Baal Thrz*, of which Mr. SWINTON makes *Baal Tarz*, and translates *Jupiter of Tarsus*; whence he concludes that this Coin was struck at that city. But the first letter of the last word is not a *Teth*, but a *Thau*, or aspirated T; and, as the Phœnicians had a vowel answering to the Roman A, it is probable they would have inserted it, had they intended it to be sounded: but we have no reason to believe, that they had any to express the U or Y, which must therefore be comprehended in the preceding consonant whenever the sound is expressed. Hence I conclude that the word here meant is *Thyrz* or *Thurz*, the *Thor* or *Thur* of the Celtes and Sarmatians, the *Thurra* of the Assyrians, the *Turan* of the Tyrrhenians or Etruscans, the *Taurine Bacchus* of the Greeks, and the Deity whom the Germans carried with them in the shape of a Bull, when they invaded ITALY; from whom the city of TYRE, as well as TYRRHENIA, or TUSCANY, probably took its name. His symbol the Bull, to which the name alludes, is represented on the Chair or Throne in which he sits; and his Sceptre, the emblem of his authority, rests upon it. The other word, *Baal*, was merely a title in the Phœnician language,

language signifying *God*, or *Lord*;* and used as an epithet of the Sun, as we learn from the name Baal-bec *(the City of Baal)* which the Greeks rendered Heliopolis, *(the City of the Sun)*.

Thus does this singular Medal shew the fundamental principles of the ancient Phœnician religion to be the same as those which appear to have prevailed through all the other nations of the Northern Hemisphere. Fragments of the same system every where occur, variously expressed as they were variously understood, and oftentimes merely preserved without being understood at all; the ancient reverence being continued to the symbols, when their meaning was wholly forgotten. The *hypostatical* division and *essential* unity of the Deity is one of the most remarkable parts of this system, and the farthest removed from common sense and reason; and yet this is perfectly reasonable and consistent, if considered together with the rest of it: for the emanations and personifications wer only figurative abstractions of particular modes of action and existence, of which the primary cause and original essence still continued one and the same.

 The

* *Cleric. Comm. in* 2 *Reg.* c. i. ver. 2.

The three Hypoſtaſes being thus only one Being, each Hypoſtaſis is occaſionally taken for all; as is the caſe in the paſſage of APULEIUS before cited, where ISIS deſcribes herſelf as the Univerſal Deity. In this character ſhe is repreſented by a ſmall Baſaltine Figure, of Egyptian ſculpture, at STRAWBERRY HILL, which is covered over with ſymbols of various kinds from top to bottom.* That of the Bull is placed loweſt, to ſhew that the ſtrength or power of the Creator is the foundation and ſupport of every other attribute. On her head are Towers to denote the Earth; and round her neck is hung a Crab-fiſh, which, from its power of ſpontaneouſly detaching from its body, and naturally reproducing, any limbs that are hurt or mutilated, became the ſymbol of the Productive Power of the Waters; in which ſenſe it appears on great numbers of ancient medals of various cities.† The Nutritive Power is ſignified by her

---

* A Print of one exactly the ſame is publiſhed by MONFAUCON, *Antiq. expliq.* Vol. I. Pl. xciii. Fig. 1.

† See thoſe of AGRIGENTUM, HIMERA, and CYRENE. On a ſmall one of the firſt-mentioned city, belonging to me, a Croſs, the abbreviated ſymbol of the Male Powers of Generation, approaches the mouth of the Crab, while the Cornucopia iſſues from it (ſee Plate XV. Fig. 12.): the one repreſents the Cauſe, and the other the Effect, of Fertilization.

her many Breaſts, and the Deſtructive by the Lions, which ſhe bears on her arms. Other attributes are expreſſed by various other animal ſymbols, the preciſe meaning of which I have not ſagacity ſufficient to diſcover.

This univerſality of the Goddeſs was more conciſely repreſented in other figures of her, by the myſtic inſtrument called a *Syſtrum*, which ſhe carried in her hand. PLUTARCH has given an explanation of it;* which may ſerve to ſhew, that the mode here adopted of explaining the ancient ſymbols is not founded merely upon conjecture and analogy, but alſo upon the authority of one of the moſt grave and learned of the Greeks. The Curved Top, he ſays, repreſented the Lunar Orbit, within which the creative attributes of the Deity were exerted, in giving motion to the four Elements, ſignified by the four Rattles below.† On the centre of the Curve was a Cat, the emblem of the Moon; who, from her influence on the conſtitutions of women, was ſuppoſed to preſide particularly

* *De Iſ. & Oſ.*

† See Plate IX. Fig. 17. engraved from one in the collection of R. WILBRAHAM, Eſq.

particularly over the paſſive Powers of Generation;* and below, upon the baſe, a head of ISIS or NEPTHUS; inſtead of which, upon that which I have had engraved, as well as upon many others now extant, are the Male Organs of Generation, repreſenting the Active Powers of the Creator, attributed to ISIS with the Paſſive. The clattering noiſe, and various motions of the Rattles being adopted as the ſymbols of the movement and mixture of the Elements, from which all things are produced; the ſound of Metals in general became an emblem of the ſame kind. Hence, the ringing of Bells, and clattering of Plates of Metal, were uſed in all luſtrations, ſacrifices, &c.† The title PRIAPUS, applied to the characteriſtic Attribute of the Creator, and ſometimes to the Creator himſelf, is probably a corruption of βριαπυος (clamorous or loud;) for the B and Π being both labials, the change of the one for the other is common in the Greek language. We ſtill find many ancient images of this ſymbol, with Bells attached to them,† as they were

* CIC. *de Nat. Deor.* Lib. II. c. 46.

† CLEM. ALEX. προτρ. p. 9. *Schol. in* THEOCRIT. Idyll, II. ver. 36.

§ *Bronzi dell' Hercol.* Tom. VI. Pl. 98.

were to the ſacred Robe of the High Prieſt of the Jews, in which he adminiſtered to the Creator.* The Bells in both were of a pyramidal form,† to ſhew the ætherial igneous Eſſence of the God. This form is ſtill retained in thoſe uſed in our Churches, as well as in the little ones rung by the Catholic Prieſts at the elevation of the Hoſt. The uſe of them was early adopted by the Chriſtians, in the ſame ſenſe as they were employed by the later Heathens; that is, as a charm againſt evil Dæmons;‡ for, being ſymbols of the active exertions of the creative attributes, they were properly oppoſed to the emanations of the deſtructive. The Lacedemonians uſed to beat a Pan or Kettle-drum at the death of their King,§ to aſſiſt in the emancipation of his ſoul, at the diſſolution of the body. We have a ſimilar cuſtom of tolling a Bell on ſuch occaſions; which is very generally practiſed, though the meaning of it has been long forgotten. This emancipation

* *Exod.* c. xxviii.

† *Bronzi dell' Hercol.* Tom. VI. Plate 98. MAIMONIDES *in Patrick's Commentary on Exodus,* c. xxviii.

‡ OVID. *Faſt.* Lib. V. ver. 441. *Schol. in* THEOCRIT. Idyll. II. ver. 36.

§ *Schol. in* THEOCRIT. Idyll. II. ver. 36.

emancipation of the Soul was ſuppoſed to be finally performed by Fire; which, being the viſible image and active eſſence of both the Creative and Deſtructive Powers, was very naturally thought to be the medium through which men paſſed from the preſent to a future life. The Greeks, and all the Celtic nations, accordingly, burned the bodies of the dead, as the Gentoos do at this day; while the Egyptians, among whom fuel was extremely ſcarce, placed them in pyramidal monuments, which were the ſymbols of Fire: hence come thoſe prodigious ſtructures which ſtill adorn that country. The Soul, which was to be emancipated, was the divine emanation, the vital ſpark of heavenly flame, the principle of reaſon and perception, which was perſonified into the ſamiliar Dæmon, or Genius, ſuppoſed to have the direction of each individual, and to diſpoſe him to good or evil, wiſdom or folly, and all their conſequences of proſperity and adverſity.* Hence proceeded the doctrines, ſo uniformly inculcated by HOMER and PINDAR,† of all human

---

* PINDAR. *Pyth.* V. ver. 164. SOPHOCL. *Trachin.* ver. 922. Hor. Lib. II. Epiſt. II. ver. 187.

† Ἐκ Θεῶν μαχαναὶ πᾶσαι βροτέαις ἀρεταῖς, καὶ σοφοὶ, καὶ χερσὶ βιαταὶ, περίγλωσσοί τ' ἔφυν. PINDAR. *Pyth.* I. ver. 79. Paſſages to the ſame purpoſe occur in almoſt every page of the *Iliad* and *Odyſſey*.

human actions depending immediately upon the Gods; which were adopted, with scarcely any variations, by some of the Christian Divines of the Apostolic age. In the Pastor of HERMAS, and Recognitions of CLEMENS, we find the Angels of Justice, Penitence, and Sorrow, instead of the Genii or Dæmons, which the ancients supposed to direct men's minds, and inspire them with those particular sentiments. St. PAUL adopted the still more comfortable doctrine of Grace, which served full as well to emancipate the consciences of the Faithful from the shackles of practical Morality. The familiar Dæmons, or divine Emanations, were supposed to reside in the Blood; which was thought to contain the principles of vital heat, and was therefore forbidden by MOSES.* HOMER, who seems to have collected little fragments of the ancient Theology, and introduced them here and there, amidst the wild profusion of his poetical fables, represents the Shades of the deceased as void of perception, until they had tasted of the blood of the victims offered by ULYSSES;† from which their faculties were renewed

* *Levit.* c. xvii. ver. 11 & 14. † *Odyss.* λ. ver. 152.

newed by a reunion with the Divine Emanation, from which they had been ſeparated. The Soul of TIRESIAS is ſaid to be entire in Hell, and to poſſeſs alone the power of perception, becauſe with him this Divine Emanation ſtill remained. The Shade of HERCULES is deſcribed among the other Ghoſts, though he himſelf, as the Poet ſays, was then in Heaven; that is, the active principle of Thought and Perception returned to its native Heaven, whilſt the Paſſive, or merely Senſitive, remained on Earth, from whence it ſprung.* The final ſeparation of theſe two, did not take place till the body was conſumed by Fire, as appears from the Ghoſt of ELPENOR, whoſe body being ſtill entire, he retained both, and knew ULYSSES before he had taſted of the Blood. It was from producing this ſeparation, that the Univerſal BACCHUS, or Double APOLLO, the Creator and Deſtroyer, whoſe eſſence was Fire, was alſo called Λικνιτης, the Purifier,† by a metaphor taken from the Winnow, which purified the Corn from the

---

* Thoſe who wiſh to ſee the difference between Senſation and Perception clearly and fully explained, may be ſatisfied by reading the *Eſſai analytique ſur l'Ame*, by Mr. BONNET.

† *Orph. Hymn.* 45.

the Duſt and Chaff, as Fire purified the Soul from its terreſtrial Pollutions. Hence this inſtrument is called by VIRGIL the Myſtic Winnow of BACCHUS.* The Ammonian Platonics, and Gnoſtic Chriſtians, thought that this ſeparation, or purification, might be effected in a degree even before death. It was for this purpoſe that they practiſed ſuch rigid temperance, and gave themſelves up to ſuch intenſe ſtudy; for, by ſubduing and extenuating the Terreſtrial Principle, they hoped to give liberty and vigour to the Celeſtial, ſo that it might be enabled to aſcend directly to the Intellectual World, pure and unincumbered.† The Clergy afterwards introduced Purgatory, inſtead of abſtract meditation and ſtudy; which was the ancient mode of ſeparation by Fire, removed into an unknown country, where it was ſaleable to all ſuch of the inhabitants of this world, as had ſufficient wealth and credulity.

It was the Celeſtial or Ætherial Principle of the Human Mind, which the ancient Artiſts repre-

 ſented

* *Myſtica vannus Iacchi.* Georg. I. ver. 166.

† PLOTIN. *Ennead.* VI. Lib. iv. c. 16. MOSHEIM, *Not.* y *in* CUDW. *Syſt. Intell.* c. v. ſect. 20.

ſented under the ſymbol of the Butterfly, which may be conſidered as one of the moſt elegant Allegories of their elegant Religion. This Inſect, when hatched from the Egg, appears in the ſhape of a Grub, crawling upon the Earth, and feeding upon the leaves of Plants. In this ſtate, it was aptly made the emblem of Man, in his earthly form, in which the ætherial vigour and activity of the Celeſtial Soul, the *divinæ particula mentis*, was ſuppoſed to be clogged and incumbered with the material body. When the Grub was changed to a Chryſalis, its ſtillneſs, torpor, and inſenſibility ſeemed to preſent a natural image of Death, or the intermediate ſtate between the ceſſation of the vital functions of the body, and the final releaſement of the ſoul by the fire, in which the body was conſumed. The Butterfly breaking from the torpid Chryſalis, and mounting in the air, was no leſs natural an image of the celeſtial Soul burſting from the reſtraints of Matter, and mixing again with its native Æther. The Greek Artiſts, always ſtudious of elegance, changed this, as well as other animal ſymbols, into a human form, retaining the Wings as the characteriſtic members, by which the meaning might be known. The Human Body, which they

added

added to them, is that of a beautiful Girl, ſometimes in the age of infancy, and ſometimes of approaching maturity. So beautiful an allegory as this would naturally be a favourite ſubject of art among a people whoſe taſte had attained the utmoſt pitch of refinement. We accordingly find that it has been more frequently and more variouſly repeated than any other, which the Syſtem of Emanations, ſo favourable to art, could afford.

Although all men were ſuppoſed to partake of the Divine Emanation in a degree, it was not ſuppoſed that they all partook of it in an equal degree. Thoſe who ſhewed ſuperior abilities, and diſtinguiſhed themſelves by their ſplendid actions, were ſuppoſed to have a larger ſhare of the Divine Eſſence, and were therefore adored as Gods, and honoured with divine titles, expreſſive of that particular Attribute of the Deity, with which they ſeemed to be moſt favoured. New perſonages were thus enrolled among the Allegorical Deities; and the perſonified Attributes of the Sun were confounded with a Cretan and Theſſalian King, an Aſiatic Conqueror, and a Theban Robber. Hence PINDAR, who appears to have been a very orthodox Heathen, ſays, that the

the race of Men and Gods is one, that both breathe from one Mother, and only differ in power.* This confusion of epithets and titles contributed, as much as any thing, to raise that vast and extravagant fabric of Poetical Mythology, which, in a manner, overwhelmed the ancient Theology, which was too pure and philosophical to continue long a popular religion. The grand and exalted system of a general First Cause, universally expanded, did not suit the gross conceptions of the multitude; who had no other way of conceiving the idea of an omnipotent God, but by forming an exaggerated image of their own Despot, and supposing his power to consist in an unlimited gratification of his passions and appetites. Hence the Universal JUPITER, the Awful and Venerable, the general Principle of Life and Motion, was transformed into the God who thundered from Mount IDA, and was lulled to sleep in the embraces of his Wife; and hence the God whose spirit moved† upon

* *Nem.* V. ver. 1.

† So the Translators have rendered the expression of the Original, which literally means brooding as a Fowl on its Eggs, and alludes to the symbols of the ancient Theology, which I have before observed upon. See PATRICK's *Commentary*.

upon the face of the Waters, and impregnated them with the Powers of Generation, became a great King above all Gods, who led forth his people to ſmite the ungodly, and rooted out their enemies from before them.

Another great means of corrupting the ancient Theology, and eſtabliſhing the Poetical Mythology, was the practice of the Artiſts in repreſenting the various attributes of the Creator under human forms of various character and expreſſion. Theſe figures, being diſtinguiſhed by the titles of the Deity which they were meant to repreſent, became in time to be conſidered as diſtinct perſonages, and worſhipped as ſeparate ſubordinate Deities. Hence the many-ſhaped God, the Πολυμορφος, and Μυριομορφος of the ancient Theologiſts, became divided into many Gods and Goddeſſes, often deſcribed by the Poets as at variance with each other, and wrangling about the little intrigues and paſſions of men. Hence too, as the ſymbols were multiplied, particular ones loſt their dignity; and that venerable one which is the ſubject of this Diſcourſe, became degraded from the repreſentative of the God of Nature to a ſubordinate rural Deity, a ſuppoſed ſon of the Aſiatic Conqueror BAC-

CHUS,

CHUS, ſtanding among the Nymphs by a Fountain,* and expreſſing the fertility of a Garden, inſtead of the general Creative Power of the great Active Principle of the Univerſe. His degradation did not ſtop even here; for we find him, in times ſtill more prophane and corrupt, made a ſubject of raillery and inſult, as anſwering no better purpoſe than holding up his rubicund ſnout to frighten the birds and thieves.† His talents were alſo perverted from their natural ends, and employed in baſe and abortive efforts in conformity to the taſte of the times; for men naturally attribute their own paſſions and inclinations to the objects of their adoration; and as God made Man in his own image, ſo Man returns the favour, and makes God in his. Hence we find the higheſt attribute of the all-pervading Spirit and firſt-begotten Love foully proſtituted to promiſcuous vice, and calling out, *Hæc cunnum, caput hic, præbeat ille nates.*‡

He continued however ſtill to have his Temple, Prieſteſs and ſacred Geeſe §, and offerings of the moſt exquiſite

* THEOCRIT. Idyll. I. ver. 21.

† HORAT. L. I. Sat. viii. VIRG. *Georg.* iv.

‡ PRIAP. Carm. 21.

§ PETRON. *Satyric.*

exquiſite kind were made to him.

Criſſabitque tibi excuſſis pulcherrima lumbis
Hoc anno primum experta puella virum.

Sometimes however they were not ſo ſcrupulous in the ſelection of their Victims, but ſuffered frugality to reſtrain their devotion.

Cum ſacrum fieret Deo ſalaci
Conducta eſt pretio puella parvo.*

The Bride was uſually placed upon him immediately before marriage; not, as LACTANTIUS ſays, *ut ejus pudicitiam prior Deus prælibaſſe videatur*, but that ſhe might be rendered fruitful by her communion with the Divine Nature, and capable of fulfilling the duties of her ſtation. In an ancient Poem† we find a Lady of the name of LALAGE preſenting the pictures of the *Elephantis* to him, and gravely requeſting that ſhe might enjoy the pleaſures over which he particularly preſided, in all the attitudes deſcribed in that celebrated Treatiſe.‡ Whether or not ſhe ſucceeded, the

Z Poet

* PRIAP. *Carm.* 34.

† PRIAP. *Carm.* 3.

‡ The *Elephantis* was written by one PHILÆNIS, and ſeems to have been of the ſame kind with the *Puttana errante* of ARRETIN.

Poet has not informed us; but we may safely conclude, that she did not trust wholly to Faith and Prayer; but, contrary to the usual practice of modern devotees, accompanied her devotion with such good Works as were likely to contribute to the end proposed by it.

When a Lady had served as the Victim in a Sacrifice to this God, she expressed her gratitude for the Benefits received, by offering upon his altar certain small images, representing his characteristic attribute; the number of which was equal to the number of Men who had acted as Priests upon the occasion.* On an antique gem, in the collection of Mr. TOWNLEY, is one of these fair Victims, who appears just returned from a sacrifice of this kind, and devoutly returning her thanks, by offering upon an altar some of these images; from the number of which, one may observe that she has not been neglected.† This offering of thanks had also its mystic and allegorical meaning; for Fire being the energetic principle and essential force of the Creator, and the symbol above

* PRIAP. *Carm.* 34. *Ed. Scioppii.* † See Plate III. Fig. 3.

above mentioned, the visible image of his characteristic Attribute, the uniting them was uniting the Material with the Essential Cause, from whose joint operation all things were supposed to proceed.

These sacrifices, as well as all those to the Deities presiding over Generation, were performed by night: hence HIPPOLYTUS, in EURIPIDES, says, to express his love of chastity, that he likes none of the Gods revered by night.* These acts of devotion were indeed attended with such rites as must naturally shock the prejudices of a chaste and temperate mind, not liable to be warmed by that ecstatic enthusiasm which is peculiar to devout persons, when their attention is absorbed in the contemplation of the beneficent Powers of the Creator, and all their faculties directed to imitate him in the exertion of his great characteristic Attribute. To heighten this enthusiasm, the Male and Female Saints of antiquity used to lie promiscuously together in the temples, and honour God by a liberal display and general communication of his bounties.† HERODOTUS, indeed, excepts the

* V. 613. † HERODOT. L. II.

Greeks and Egyptians, and DIONYSIUS of HALICARNASSUS the Romans, from this general cuſtom of other nations: but to the teſtimony of the former we may oppoſe the thouſand ſacred Proſtitutes kept at each of the Temples of CORINTH and ERYX;* and to that of the latter, the expreſs words of JUVENAL, who, though he lived an age later, lived when the ſame religion, and nearly the ſame manners, prevailed.† DIODORUS SICULUS alſo tells us, that when the Roman Prætors viſited ERYX, they laid aſide their magiſterial ſeverity, and honoured the Goddeſs by mixing with her votaries, and indulging themſelves in the pleaſures over which ſhe preſided.‡ It appears too, that the act of Generation was a ſort of ſacrament in the Iſland of LESBOS; for the device on its medals, (which in the Greek republics had always ſome relation to religion) is as explicit as forms can make it.§ The figures appear indeed to be myſtic and allegorical, the Male having evidently a mixture of

* STRAB. Lib. VIII.

† *Sat.* IX. ver. 24.

‡ Lib. IV. *Ed. Weſſel.*

§ See Plate IX. Fig. 5. from one belonging to me.

of the Goat in his beard and features, and therefore probably repreſents PAN, the Generative Power of the Univerſe, incorporated in univerſal matter. The Female has all that breadth and fulneſs which characteriſe the perſonification of the paſſive Power, known by the tiles of RHEA, JUNO, CERES, &c.

When there were ſuch ſeminaries for female education as thoſe of ERYX and CORINTH, we need not wonder that the Ladies of antiquity ſhould be extremely well inſtructed in all the practical duties of their religion. The ſtories told of JULIA and MESSALINA ſhew us that the Roman Ladies were no ways deficient; and yet they were as remarkable for their gravity and decency, as the Corinthians were for their ſkill and dexterity in adapting themſelves to all the modes and attitudes, which the luxuriant imaginations of experienced Votaries have contrived for performing the rites of their tutelar Goddeſs.*

The reaſon why theſe rites were always performed by Night, was the peculiar ſanctity attributed to it by the Ancients, becauſe dreams were then ſuppoſed to deſcend

* PHILODEMI *Epigr. Brunk. Analect.* Vol. II. p. 85.

ſcend from heaven to inſtruct and forewarn men. The Nights, ſays HESIOD, belong to the bleſſed Gods;* and the Orphic Poet calls night the ſource of all things, (παντων γενετις) to denote that productive power, which, as I have been told, it really poſſeſſes; it being obſerved that plants and animals grow more by night than by day. The ancients extended this power much farther, and ſuppoſed, that not only the productions of the earth, but the luminaries of heaven, were nouriſhed and ſuſtained by the benign influence of the night. Hence that beautiful apoſtrophe in the *Electra* of EURIPIDES, Ω νυξ μελαινα, χρυσεων αστρων τροφε, &c.

Not only the ſacrifices to the Generative Deities, but in general all the religious rites of the Greeks, were of the feſtive kind. To imitate the Gods, was in their opinion to feaſt and rejoice, and to cultivate the uſeful and elegant arts, by which we are made partakers of their felicity.† This was the caſe with almoſt all the nations of antiquity, except the ‡Egyptians

* Εργ. ver. 730. † STRABO, Lib. X.

‡ HERODOT. Lib. II.

tians, and their reformed imitators the Jews,* who, being governed by a Hierarchy, endeavoured to make it aweful and venerable to the people, by an appearance of rigour and austerity. The people however sometimes broke through this restraint, and indulged themselves in the more pleasing worship of their neighbours, as when they danced and feasted before the Golden Calf which AARON erected,† and devoted themselves to the worship of obscene Idols, generally supposed to be of PRIAPUS, under the reign of ABIJAM.‡

The Christian religion, being a reformation of the Jewish, rather increased than diminished the austerity of its original. On particular occasions however it equally abated its rigour, and gave way to festivity and mirth, though always with an air of sanctity and solemnity. Such were originally the feasts of the Eucharist, which, as the Word expresses, were meetings of joy and gratulation; though, as Divines tell us, all of the spiritual kind: but the particular manner in which St. AUGUSTINE commands the Ladies who

* See SPENCER *de Leg. Rit. Vet. Hebræor.* † *Exod.* c. xxxii.

‡ *Reg.* c. xv. ver. 13. *Ed. Cleric.*

who attended them to wear clean linen,* ſeems to infer, that perſonal as well as ſpiritual matters were thought worthy of attention. To thoſe who adminiſter the Sacrament in the modern way, it may appear of little conſequence whether the Woman received it in clean linen or not; but to the good Biſhop, who was to adminiſter the *holy Kiſs*, it certainly was of ſome importance. The *holy Kiſs* was not only applied as a part of the ceremonial of the Euchariſt, but alſo of Prayer, at the concluſion of which they welcomed each other with this natural ſign of Love and Benevolence.† It was upon theſe occaſions that they worked themſelves up to thoſe fits of rapture and enthuſiaſm, which made them eagerly ruſh upon deſtruction in the fury of their zeal to obtain the crown of Martyrdom.‡ Enthuſiaſm on one ſubject naturally produces enthuſiaſm on another; for the human paſſions, like the ſtrings of an inſtrument, vibrate to the motions of each other: hence paroxyſms of Love and Devotion have oftentimes ſo exactly accorded, as not to have been diſtinguiſhed

* AUG. *Serm.* clii. † JUSTIN MARTYR. *Apolog.*

‡ MARTINI KEMPII *de Oſculis Diſſert.* VIII.

diſtinguiſhed by the very perſons whom they agitated.* This was too often the caſe in theſe meetings of the primitive Chriſtians. The feaſts of Gratulation and Love, the αγαπαι and nocturnal vigils, gave too flattering opportunities to the paſſions and appetites of men, to continue long, what we are told they were at firſt, pure exerciſes of devotion. The ſpiritual raptures and divine ecſtaſies encouraged on theſe occaſions, were often ecſtaſies of a very different kind, concealed under the garb of devotion; whence the greateſt irregularities enſued; and it became neceſſary for the reputation of the Church, that they ſhould be ſuppreſſed, as they afterwards were, by the decrees of ſeveral Councils. Their ſuppreſſion may be conſidered as the final ſubverſion of that part of the ancient religion, which I have here undertaken to examine; for ſo long as theſe nocturnal meetings were preſerved, it certainly exiſted, though under other names, and in a more ſolemn dreſs. The ſmall remain of it preſerved at Isernia, of which an account has here been given, can ſcarcely be deemed an exception; for its meaning was un-

* See *Procès de la Cadière.*

known to thofe who celebrated it; and the obfcurity of the place, added to the venerable names of St. COSIMO and DAMIANO, was all that prevented it from being fuppreffed long ago, as it has been lately, to the great difmay of the chafte Matrons and pious Monks of ISERNIA. Traces and memorials of it feem however to have been preferved, in many parts of Chriftendom, long after the actual celebration of its rites ceafed. Hence the obfcene figures obfervable upon many of our Gothic Cathedrals, and particularly upon the ancient brafs doors of St. PETER's at ROME, where there are fome groupes which rival the devices on the Lefbian medals.

It is curious, in looking back through the annals of fuperftition, fo degrading to the pride of man, to trace the progrefs of the human mind in different ages, climates, and circumftances, uniformly acting upon the fame principles, and to the fame ends. The fketch here given of the corruptions of the religion of GREECE, is an exact counterpart of the hiftory of the corruptions of Chriftianity, which began in the pure Theifm of the Eclectic Jews,* and

* Compare the doctrines of PHILO with thofe taught in the *Gofpel of* St. JOHN, and *Epiftles of* St. PAUL.

and by the help of Inſpirations, Emanations, and Canonizations, expanded itſelf, by degrees, to the vaſt and unwieldy ſyſtem which now fills the Creed of what is commonly called the Catholic Church. In the ancient religion, however, the Emanations aſſumed the appearance of Moral Virtues and Phyſical Attributes, inſtead of miniſtering Spirits and guardian Angels; and the canonizations or deifications were beſtowed upon Heroes, Legiſlators, and Monarchs, inſtead of Prieſts, Monks, and Martyrs. There is alſo this further difference, that among the moderns Philoſophy has improved, as Religion has been corrupted; whereas, among the ancients, Religion and Philoſophy declined together. The true Solar Syſtem was taught in the Orphic School, and adopted by the Pythagoreans, the next regularly-eſtabliſhed ſect. The Stoics corrupted it a little, by placing the Earth in the centre of the univerſe, though they ſtill allowed the Sun its ſuperior magnitude.* At length aroſe the Epicureans, who confounded it entirely, maintaining that the Sun was only a ſmall globe of fire, a few inches in diameter,

* Brucker, *Hiſt. Crit. Philoſ.* P. II. Lib. II. c. 9. ſ. 1.

and the Stars little tranſitory lights, whirled about in the atmoſphere of the Earth.*

How ill ſoever adapted the ancient ſyſtem of Emanations was, to procure eternal happineſs, it was certainly extremely well calculated to produce temporal good; for, by the endleſs multiplication of ſubordinate Deities, it effectually excluded two of the greateſt curſes that ever afflicted the human race, Dogmatical Theology, and its conſequent Religious Perſecution. Far from ſuppoſing that the Gods known in their own country were the only ones exiſting, the Greeks thought that innumerable Emanations of the Divine Mind were diffuſed through every part of the univerſe; ſo that new objects of devotion preſented themſelves wherever they went. Every mountain, ſpring, and river, had its tutelary deity, beſides the numbers of immortal ſpirits that were ſuppoſed to wander in the air, ſcattering dreams and viſions, and ſuperintending the affairs of men.

> Τρις γαρ μυριοι εισιν επι χθονι πουλυβοτειρη
> Αθανατοι Ζηνος, φυλακες θνητων ανθρωπων.†

An

* Lucret. Lib. V. ver. 565. & ſeq.

† Hesiod. Εργα και Ημερ. ver. 252. μυριοι, &c. are always uſed as undefinites by the ancient Greek Poets.

An adequate knowledge of theſe they never preſumed to think attainable, but modeſtly contented themſelves with revering and invoking them whenever they felt, or wanted their aſſiſtance. When a ſhipwrecked Mariner was caſt upon an unknown coaſt, he immediately offered up his prayers to the Gods of the country, whoever they were; and joined the inhabitants in whatever rites they thought proper to propitiate them with.* Impious or prophane rites he never imagined could exiſt, concluding, that all expreſſions of gratitude and ſubmiſſion muſt be pleaſing to the Gods. Atheiſm was, indeed, puniſhed at ATHENS, as the obſcene ceremonies of the Bacchanalians were at ROME; but both as civil crimes againſt the State; the one tending to weaken the bands of ſociety by deſtroying the ſanctity of oaths, and the other to ſubvert that decency and gravity of manners, upon which the Romans ſo much prided themſelves. The introduction of ſtrange Gods, without permiſſion from the Magiſtrate, was alſo prohibited

* See HOMER. *Odyſſ.* ι, ver. 445, & ſeq. The Greeks ſeem to have adopted by degrees into their own Ritual all the rites practiſed in the neighbouring countries.

hibited in both cities; but the reſtriction extended no farther than the walls, there being no other parts of the Roman Empire, except JUDÆA, in which any kind of impiety or extravagance might not have been maintained with impunity, provided it was maintained merely as a ſpeculative opinion, and not employed as an engine of Faction, Ambition, or Oppreſſion. The Romans even carried their condeſcenſion ſo far as to enforce the obſervance of a Dogmatical Religion, where they found it before eſtabliſhed; as appears from the conduct of their Magiſtrates in Judea, relative to CHRIST and his Apoſtles; and from what JOSEPHUS has related, of a Roman Soldier's being puniſhed with death by his Commander, for inſulting the Books of MOSES. Upon what principle then did they act, when they afterwards perſecuted the Chriſtians with ſo much rancour and cruelty? Perhaps it may ſurpriſe perſons not uſed to the ſtudy of eccleſiaſtical antiquities, to be told (what is nevertheleſs indiſputably true) that the Chriſtians were never perſecuted on account of the ſpeculative opinions of individuals, but either for civil crimes laid to their charge, or for withdrawing their allegiance from the State, and joining in a federative union dangerous by its conſtitution, and rendered

dered ſtill more dangerous by the intolerant principles of its members, who often tumultuouſly interrupted the public worſhip, and continually railed againſt the national religion (with which both the civil government and military diſcipline of the Romans were inſeparably connected), as the certain means of eternal damnation. To break this Union, was the great object of Roman policy during a long courſe of years; but the violent means employed only tended to cement it cloſer. Some of the Chriſtians themſelves indeed, who were addicted to Platoniſm, took a ſafer method to diſſolve it; but they were too few in number to ſucceed. This was by trying to moderate that furious zeal which gave life and vigour to the confederacy, and to blend and ſoften the unyielding temper of Religion with the mild ſpirit of Philoſophy. "We all," ſaid they, "agree in worſhipping one Supreme God, the Father "and Preſerver of all. While we approach him "with purity of mind, ſincerity of heart, and inno"cence of manners, forms and ceremonies of wor"ſhip are indifferent; and not leſs worthy of his "greatneſs, for being varied and diverſified according "to the various cuſtoms and opinions of men. Had "it been his will that all ſhould have worſhipped

"him

"him in the ſame mode, he would have given to "all the ſame inclinations and conceptions: but he "has wiſely ordered it otherwiſe, that Piety and Virtue "might increaſe by an honeſt emulation of religions, "as induſtry in trade, or activity in a race, from the "mutual emulation of the candidates for wealth and "honour.* This was too liberal and extenſive a plan, to meet the approbation of a greedy and ambitious Clergy, whoſe object was to eſtabliſh a Hierarchy for themſelves, rather than to procure happineſs for others. It was accordingly condemned with vehemence and ſucceſs by AMBROSIUS, PRUDENTIUS, and other orthodox leaders of the age.

It was from the ancient ſyſtem of Emanations, that the general hoſpitality which characteriſed the manners of the heroic ages, and which is ſo beautifully repreſented in the *Odyſſey* of HOMER, in a great meaſure aroſe. The poor, and the ſtranger who wandered in the ſtreet, and begged at the door, were ſuppoſed to be animated by a portion of the ſame Divine Spirit which ſuſtained the great and powerful.

They

---

* SYMMACH. *Ep.* 10 & 61. THEMIST. *Orat ad Imperat.*

They are all from Jupiter, says HOMER, *and a ſmall gift is acceptable.** This benevolent ſentiment has been compared by the Engliſh Commentators to that of the Jewiſh Moraliſt, who ſays, *that he who giveth to the poor lendeth to the Lord, who will repay him ten-fold.*† But it is ſcarcely poſſible for any thing to be more different: HOMER promiſes no other reward for charity than the benevolence of the action itſelf; but the Iſraelite holds out that, which has always been the great motive for charity among his countrymen—the proſpect of being repaid ten-fold. They are always ready to ſhow their bounty upon ſuch incentives, if they can be perſuaded that they are founded upon good ſecurity. It was the opinion, however, of many of the moſt learned among the ancients, that the principles of the Jewiſh religion were originally the ſame as thoſe of the Greek, and that their God was no other than the Creator and Generator BACCHUS,‡ who, being viewed through the gloomy medium of the hierarchy, appeared to them a jealous and iraſcible God; and ſo gave

* *Odyſ.* ζ. ver. 207. † See POPE's *Odyſſey.* ‡ TACIT. *Hiſtor.* Lib. v.

a more auſtere and unſociable form to their devotion. The Golden Vine preſerved in the Temple at Jeruſalem,* and the Taurine forms of the Cherubs, between which the Deity was ſuppoſed to reſide, were ſymbols ſo exactly ſimilar to their own, that they naturally concluded them meant to expreſs the ſame ideas; eſpecially as there was nothing in the avowed principles of the Jewiſh worſhip to which they could be applied. The ineffable name alſo, which, according to the Maſſorethic punctuation, is pronounced *Jehovah*, was anciently pronounced *Jaho*, Ιαω, or Ιευω,† which was a title of BACCHUS, the nocturnal Sun;‡ as was alſo *Sabazius*, or *Sabadius*,§ which is the ſame word as *Sabbaoth*, one of the ſcriptural titles of the true God, only adapted to the pronunciation of a more poliſhed language. The Latin name for the Supreme God belongs alſo to the ſame root; Ιυ-πατηρ, JUPITER, ſignifying Father Ιυ', though written after the ancient manner,

---

* The Vine and Goblet of BACCHUS are alſo the uſual devices upon the Jewiſh and Samaritan Coins, which were ſtruck under the Aſmonean Kings.

† HIERON. *Comm. in Pſalm.* VIII. DIODOR. SIC. Lib. I. PHILO-BYBL. *ap. Euſeb. Prep. Evang.* Lib. I. c. ix.

‡ MACROB. *Sat.* Lib. I. c. xviii. § Ibid.

manner, without the diphthong, which was not in uſe for many ages after the Greek Colonies ſettled in LATIUM, and introduced the Arcadian Alphabet. We find St. PAUL likewiſe acknowledging, that the JUPITER of the Poet ARATUS was the God whom he adored ;* and CLEMENS of ALEXANDRIA explains St. PETER's prohibition of worſhipping after the manner of the Greeks, not to mean a prohibition of worſhipping the ſame God, but merely of the corrupt mode in which he was then worſhipped.†

---

* *Act. Apoſt.* Chap. xvii. ver. 28. † STROMAT. Lib. V.

THE END.

www.ingramcontent.com/pod-product-compliance
Lightning Source LLC
Chambersburg PA
CBHW030326270326
41926CB00010B/1520
* 9 7 8 3 3 3 7 2 7 3 5 6 9 *